GO NUTS

Go Nuts

RECIPES THAT REALLY SHELL OUT

DEBBIE HARDING

TouchWood
Editions

TouchWood Editions
www.touchwoodeditions.com

Library and Archives Canada Cataloguing in Publication
Harding, Debbie, 1956–
   Go nuts : recipes that really shell out / Debbie Harding.

Includes index.
ISBN 978-1-926741-11-6
   1. Cookery (Nuts). I. Title.

TX814.H37 2010   641.6'45   C2010-903675-1

Editor: Holland Gidney
Cover design: Pete Kohut
Cover and interior illustrations: Debbie Harding
Author photo: Doug Harding

 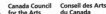

BRITISH COLUMBIA ARTS COUNCIL
Supported by the Province of British Columbia

Canada Council for the Arts   Conseil des Arts du Canada

We gratefully acknowledge the financial support for our publishing activities from the Government of Canada through the Canada Book Fund, Canada Council for the Arts, and the province of British Columbia through the British Columbia Arts Council and the Book Publishing Tax Credit.

Mixed Sources
Cert no. SW-COC-001271
© 1996 FSC
FSC

The interior pages of this book have been printed on 100% post-consumer recycled paper, processed chlorine free, and printed with vegetable-based inks.

1 2 3 4 5 13 12 11 10

PRINTED IN CANADA

Go Nuts, being my first cookbook, is dedicated to two very important people:

To Doug, my husband, who has been there for me and participated in every adventure of mine, personally and in business. He is the best husband and friend (and business partner) anyone could ask for. He is my biggest fan and a careful but honest critic who has survived my extensive food experiments over the years. I absolutely love cooking and creating art illustrations. I could not do either professionally, let alone both, without his endless support and encouragement.

And to my mom, who is no longer here but is always in my heart. She nurtured my love of cooking and baking at an early age and always allowed me to participate. Preparing food was never a chore but an interesting project or creation. She expanded her knowledge of cooking by taking classes and trying new recipes, which made our family meals satisfying and delicious. I wish I could share this book with her because she would be very excited and proud.

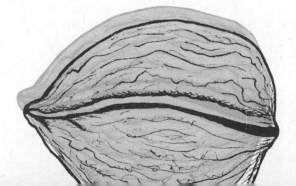

Table of Contents

Foreword

My wife and I have been aware of Debbie's inventive and delicious culinary activities for many years, dating back to when she catered our daughter's wedding 15 years ago. Over the years, she also prepared food for family trips to our summer house on Denman Island. We were happy to learn Debbie was finally writing a cookbook to share her delicious recipes with others; selecting nuts as her focus is an interesting, tasty, and healthy choice.

Nuts come from all over the world, from places with climates ranging from the temperate to the tropical. Because they are usually the seeds of a variety of trees, covered with a hard shell, it is not surprising that they contain a full range of important nutrition constituents. Nuts include Omega-3 fatty acids, which the body needs to protect good cholesterol, plus proteins, vitamins, and trace elements. Some nuts, like Brazil nuts, macadamia nuts, and cashews, contain larger quantities of saturated fat and are therefore best consumed in smaller quantities. The vitamin content (B, B2, B6, C, and E) and elemental content (copper, magnesium, selenium, iron, and manganese) of nuts also varies considerably, which is a good reason to consume a variety of nuts for optimal health benefits. Finally, the high selenium content of Brazil nuts may soon be of added importance if studies now underway confirm selenium to be important in the prevention of prostate cancer.

—Dr. Peter Coy, retired radiologist and former director of the Victoria Cancer Clinic

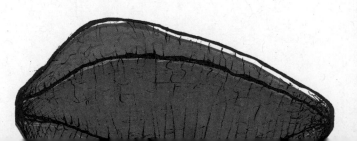

A Message from the Author

My favourite cookbooks are the ones that are stained and falling apart. The coffee-table books that I own sit on the shelf and are glanced at about once per year; they have pretty pictures but are not handy to use nor do they have any appropriate recipes for everyday meals or for entertaining family and friends. I wanted *Go Nuts* to be different. Because nuts are so versatile, I'm confident this cookbook will become one you use often. I encourage you to spill on it, flag the pages, and wear it out well. Like my favourite cookbooks, I hope your copy of *Go Nuts* is one day held together with an elastic band.

While researching nuts for this cookbook, I realized that many "nuts" are not actually nuts at all. Most people know that peanuts are not nuts but actually pods from a legume, which is why some people refer to them as "groundnuts" or "earthnuts" to differentiate them from nuts grown on trees. (Although, if you ask someone what is the most common nut allergy, most people would answer peanuts!) A true nut is the edible, single-seed kernel of a fruit surrounded by a hard shell. Hazelnuts, pecans, chestnuts, and macadamias match that description but other "nuts" do not. For instance, walnuts have two kernels so they are not technically nuts. An almond is actually a drupe and Brazil nuts, cashews, and pine nuts are technically seeds. But for most recipes, including the ones included in this book, a nut is any fruit or seed with an edible kernel surrounded by a hard shell. As a result, coconut teeters on the "is it a nut?" border for me, which is why I have included several recipes with coconut in them but, because many people do not think of it as a nut, I do not focus on it as a feature ingredient or flavour. For practical reasons, *Go Nuts* uses only familiar nuts, not the unusual ones. It was difficult to decide on the recipes for this cookbook because there are so many great ideas for nuts, and I could easily write one or two books just on desserts made with nuts. In the end, I decided to focus on the most common nuts that are readily available: almonds, Brazil nuts, cashews, chestnuts, hazelnuts, macadamia nuts, peanuts, pecans, pine nuts, pistachios, and walnuts.

Go Nuts includes new and unique recipes as well as some classics. For example, Chocolate Almond Ganache (p. 131) is the very successful result of an experiment to create a dairy-free ganache while Hazelnut Hollandaise (p. 6) is a variation of the classic sauce made using an easy food processor method. With so many options for incorporating different types of nuts into your diet, you'll soon go nuts for nuts.

Enjoy!

—Debbie Harding

Breakfast, Breads, and Baked Goods

Baked Mushroom and Almond Omelettes

These omelettes can be prepared the day before, brought to room temperature, and then baked to serve.

Preheat the oven to 375°F (190°C) and oil four round 4-inch (10 cm) ramekins.

Filling

Heat the olive oil in a large skillet on medium-high heat. Add the mushrooms and cook them until they are light golden and the moisture is gone. Add the lemon juice and the seasoning; mix well. Remove from heat and add the almonds. Set aside.

Omelettes

In a large bowl, whisk the eggs with the water and the seasoning. Heat a large, non-stick, oiled skillet on medium heat. Add the egg mixture and loosely scramble the eggs until only half-cooked. This step will take 2 to 3 minutes; eggs should be semi-solid but remain very wet.

Filling

1 Tbsp (15 mL) olive oil

½ lb (250 g) mushrooms, sliced ¼-inch (6 mm) thick

1 tsp (5 mL) lemon juice

¼ tsp (1 mL) garlic salt

¼ tsp (1 mL) pepper

½ cup (125 mL) toasted flaked almonds (or substitute chopped walnuts, pecans, or hazelnuts)

Omelettes

12 large eggs

¼ cup (60 mL) water

½ tsp (2 mL) salt

½ tsp (2 mL) pepper

1 cup (250 mL) grated aged or sharp cheddar

dried parsley or paprika for garnishing

vegetable oil for ramekins

Serves 4.

Per serving: 505 cals, 38.8 g fat, 13 g sat. fat, 666 mg cholesterol, 837 mg sodium, 7.6 g carbs, 31.2 g protein

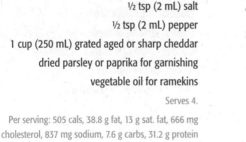

Divide half of the egg mixture between the four ramekins. Add 2 tablespoons (30 mL) of cheese to each ramekin, and then one-quarter of the mushroom–nut mixture. Divide the remaining egg mixture between the ramekins.

Top each dish with 2 tablespoons (30 mL) of cheese and sprinkle with parsley or paprika. At this point, they can be covered and refrigerated overnight. Remove from the fridge 30 minutes prior to baking. Place the ramekins on a baking sheet or into a shallow pan. Bake the omelettes until the cheese is bubbling and the eggs are set, about 10 to 15 minutes.

Garnishing

Egg dishes are pale in colour and benefit from the addition of some colour. I add a sprinkle of paprika or dried parsley to the top of each omelette before baking. If you would like to use freshly minced parsley leaves, add the garnish just before serving. If preparing omelettes ahead of time, you can add the dry garnish before covering and refrigerating them.

Benny Goes Nuts

This special version of eggs Benedict will win the hearts of all the Benny fans out there!

¼ cup (60 mL) white vinegar

8 large eggs

12 medium-thin asparagus stalks, washed, trimmed, and cut into 3- to 4-inch (8- to 10-mm) pieces

1 Tbsp (15 mL) olive oil

4 English muffins, sliced in half

8 beefsteak tomato slices, ¼ to ⅓ inch (6 to 8 mm) thick (or 12 to 16 slices if using smaller tomatoes)

1 recipe Hazelnut Hollandaise (p. 6)

Serves 4, with 2 eggs per person.

1 Eggs Benny (with sauce): 416 cals, 32.3 g fat, 15.5 g sat. fat, 411 mg cholesterol, 416 mg sodium, 18.4 g carbs, 12.5 g protein

Preheat the oven to 200°F (95°C).

Set aside a bowl of ice water. Add the vinegar to a large pot of boiling water. Reduce the heat to a simmer so it's not quite boiling.

One at a time, crack each egg into a small bowl or cup and then slide it into the water. Poach the eggs until the whites are set. Use a slotted spoon to transfer the eggs to a bowl of ice water—which will stop the cooking—rinse off the vinegar, and chill them.

In a medium skillet, cook the asparagus in the olive oil on medium heat for 3 to 4 minutes, until tender-crisp.

Toast the English muffins and place face up in the oven on a baking sheet. Top each half with tomato slices and cooked asparagus; keep warm in the oven. Have the Hazelnut Hollandaise warm and ready.

Boil a large pot of water. Place the eggs in the boiling water and reheat for 1 minute. Drain them well and then place one on top of each of the prepared English muffins halves.

Top each "Benny" with 1 to 1½ tablespoons (15 to 22.5 mL) of Hazelnut Hollandaise and serve immediately.

Poaching Eggs

Fresh, cold eggs poach the best.

Bring the water to a boil and then reduce the heat to keep it just below the boiling point. Next add the vinegar.

Crack each egg individually into a small measuring cup or bowl just before you add it to the water.

As you slide each egg into the hot water, use a wooden spoon to gently form the egg white into a round mass around the yolk while the white cooks. This helps keep it together and creates a nicely shaped poached egg. Work quickly when adding the eggs to the water to ensure that they all cook for about the same period of time.

When you add each egg to the water, increase the heat by a fraction to keep the water hot and almost boiling. If the water is boiling rapidly the whites tend to turn out rubbery so it's important to keep the water at the right temperature.

If you have several eggs in the same pot, you may not be able to tell which egg is which. Cook them for 3 minutes for runny yolks and soft-cooked whites.

If the edges are ragged after cooking, eggs can be trimmed and shaped with scissors.

Hazelnut Hollandaise

This version of Hollandaise sauce is extra special and very easy to make but it does require a food processor or blender.

3 large eggs

2 Tbsp (30 mL) lemon juice

¾ cup plus 2 Tbsp (215 mL) hot melted butter

2 Tbsp (30 mL) hazelnut butter

¾ tsp (4 mL) salt

¼ tsp (1 mL) pepper

Makes 1¼ cups (310 mL), enough for 8 servings of eggs Benedict. Leftover sauce can be used on baked potatoes as a topping (without reheating); see Baked Red Potatoes (p. 101).

Per Tbsp (15 mL): 99 cals, 10.4 g fat, 5.5 g sat. fat, 80 mg cholesterol, 98 mg sodium, 0.5 g carbs, 1.1 g protein

Place the whole eggs in a bowl of very hot water for 5 minutes. Crack the eggs and separate the yolks from the whites. Place the yolks in the bowl of a food processor (or blender); the whites can be frozen and used for another recipe. Microwave the lemon juice for 15 to 20 seconds on medium heat.

With the processor on medium to medium-high speed, add the hot lemon juice; mix well. Run a spatula around the inside edges of the bowl; pulse again to mix. Add the hazelnut butter and seasoning; pulse a few times to mix well. With the motor running, gradually add the butter; mix well until the sauce thickens. Run a spatula around the inside edges of the bowl to incorporate all the yolk mixture; mix again if needed.

Keep warm and use as soon as possible. If you need to reheat this sauce, do it very gently using a double boiler.

Maple Walnut Bacon

An excellent side dish for Sunday brunch or family breakfasts at holiday time.

Preheat the oven to 375°F (190°C) and oil a baking sheet.

In a large, oiled skillet, fry the bacon until cooked through but not browned. Drain the bacon on paper towels and then lay slices out flat on the baking sheet. Brush each slice of bacon with maple syrup and sprinkle with 1 teaspoon (5 mL) of walnut pieces.

Cook the bacon until bubbly and browned, about 5 or more minutes. Flip over each strip of bacon; brush again with maple syrup and sprinkle with another 1 teaspoon (5 mL) of nuts. Return the baking sheet to the oven to brown the second side for 4 to 5 minutes. Serve warm.

1 Tbsp (15 mL) vegetable oil
for baking sheet and skillet

12 strips of thick-slice bacon

½ cup (125 mL) maple syrup

¾ cup (185 mL) walnut pieces, finely chopped

Serves 4 people, with 3 strips of bacon per person.

Per slice: 302 cals, 23.2 g fat, 7 g sat. fat, 32 mg cholesterol, 605 mg sodium, 10.4 g carbs, 12.6 g protein

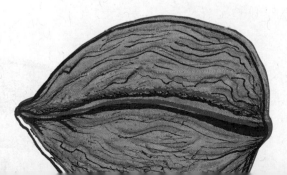

Southern Spicy Pork Sausage Patties

Since these patties freeze well, you may wish to double this recipe and freeze half before cooking. (You can also freeze them after cooking but they may be on the dry side after you reheat them.)

1 lb (500 g) ground pork
½ cup (125 mL) raw pecans, finely chopped
1 tsp (5 mL) salt
½ tsp (2 mL) pepper
¼ tsp (1 mL) cayenne pepper
1 tsp (5 mL) Chinese chili–garlic sauce
¼ tsp (1 mL) poultry seasoning
2 Tbsp (30 mL) butter
2 Tbsp (30 mL) vegetable oil

Makes 12 sausage patties.

Per patty: 152 cals, 13.5 g fat, 4 g sat. fat, 30 mg cholesterol, 226 mg sodium, 1 g carbs, 6.8 g protein

Add the meat, nuts and seasoning to a medium bowl; stir well to combine. Form 2-inch (5 cm) meatballs; flatten them to make 3-inch (8 cm) patties. Heat the oil and butter in a large, non-stick skillet on medium heat.

Add the patties and cook, covered, for about 5 minutes to brown the sausage. Turn them over gently and cook, covered, for another 5 minutes to brown the other side and cook them through. Check to see if they are cooked thoroughly. They should be firm when pressed and the juice should run clear when pierced with a fork. If they need more time to cook, turn the heat down to medium-low.

Remove from the skillet. Cover and keep warm on a plate in a 200°F (95°C) oven until ready to serve.

Pumpkin Pecan Pancakes

This recipe is a fall/winter favourite and works well for serving a crowd. You can make the pancakes the day before and reheat them, wrapped in foil, in a 350°F (180°F) oven for 10 to 15 minutes. If you make too many, they also freeze well.

Preheat the oven to 250°F (120°C), to keep cooked pancakes warm while you finish frying the rest.

Mix together the first four ingredients in a medium bowl. In a large bowl, sift together the dry ingredients; add the pecans. Make a well in the dry ingredients; pour in the wet ingredients and mix only until incorporated.

Preheat an oiled, non-stick skillet or griddle on medium-high heat. Test the skillet with a teaspoon (5 mL) of batter; it should sizzle if at the right temperature. Portion 3 tablespoons (45 mL) of batter per pancake; fry for 2 to 3 minutes or until the bottom is golden and the bubbles on top have popped. Flip over and brown the other side for 1 to 2 minutes.

Keep them warm in the oven while you fry the rest of the pancakes. Serve with maple syrup or fruit syrup on the side.

1½ cups (375 mL) canned pumpkin purée

1 large egg, beaten

1¾ cups (185 mL) milk

2 Tbsp (30 mL) melted butter

1½ cups (375 mL) flour

1 Tbsp (15 mL) baking powder

½ tsp (2 mL) salt

2 Tbsp (30 mL) sugar

1 tsp (5 mL) cinnamon

½ tsp (2 mL) nutmeg

½ tsp (2 mL) ginger

½ cup (125 mL) pecans, chopped and toasted

maple syrup or fruit syrup

Serves 6, with 4 pancakes per person.

Per serving: 320 cals, 14.3 g fat, 4.9 g sat. fat, 55 mg cholesterol, 248 mg sodium, 39.8 g carbs, 8 g protein

Apple Praline Waffles

These waffles are excellent with a bit of cinnamon sprinkled on top so they taste like apple pie.

Preheat your waffle iron according to the manufacturer's instructions. Preheat the oven to 250°F (120°C) for keeping cooked waffles warm.

In a bowl, mix all the dry ingredients, except the almonds, together; make a well in the ingredients. Stir the beaten eggs into the milk and butter, and then pour into the well, mixing only until smooth.

Referring to the manufacturer's instructions, add enough batter to the waffle iron; close the lid to cook. Cook waffles until the steam stops escaping, and the waffles are brown and crisp.

Keep waffles warm in the oven until all the batter is used up. Top waffles with warm Amaretto Apples and sprinkle with toasted almonds and cinnamon.

1½ cups (375 mL) flour
2 Tbsp (30 mL) sugar
1 Tbsp (15 mL) baking powder
½ tsp (2 mL) salt
2 large eggs, beaten
1½ cups (375 mL) milk
¼ cup (60 mL) melted butter
1 recipe Amaretto Apples (p. 10)
½ cup (125 mL) toasted, sliced blanched almonds
ground cinnamon in a shaker for garnishing

Serves 4.

Per serving: 674 cals, 33.9 g fat, 15 g sat. fat, 164 g cholesterol, 443 mg sodium, 77.2 g carbs, 15.1 g protein

Amaretto Apples

These apples are great on their own, or with crepes, waffles, pound cake, or ice cream.

In a bowl, toss the apple slices with the lemon juice. In a large, non-stick skillet on medium-high heat, melt the butter. Add the apple slices and Amaretto; sprinkle with the sugar.

Cook until caramelized and golden. After 7 to 10 minutes, the liquid will have reduced enough to form a sauce.

4 large apples, peeled, cored, and sliced ¼-inch (6 mm) thick
2 Tbsp (30 mL) lemon juice
2 Tbsp (30 mL) butter
¼ cup (60 mL) sugar
2 Tbsp (30 mL) Amaretto liqueur

Serves 4.

Per serving: 165 cals, 6.8 g fat, 4.1 g sat. fat, 16 mg cholesterol, 6 mg sodium, 25.4 g carbs, 0.4 g protein

Cinnamon Pecan French Toast

This is a great breakfast or brunch dish for over the holidays. And you prep it a day ahead!

Oil a large, rectangular baking pan.

In a medium bowl, mix the melted butter with the brown sugar, honey, and cinnamon and use it to coat the bottom of the pan; sprinkle the nuts over top.

In a small bowl, mix together the cinnamon and white sugar for the topping; set aside.

Arrange a layer of bread slices tightly in the bottom of the pan. You may have some bread left over. In a bowl, whisk the eggs. Add the cream, vanilla, liqueur, and salt; mix well. Pour over the bread, and let it soak in.

Sprinkle the bread with the cinnamon–sugar topping and the remaining nuts. Cover and chill for at least 8 hours (overnight), or up to 1½ days.

Remove the baking dish from the fridge 30 minutes prior to baking; preheat the oven to 350°F (180°C). Bake for 35 to 40 minutes. French toast should be puffy and light golden when done.

Base

vegetable oil for baking dish

½ cup (125 mL) melted butter

1 packed cup dark brown sugar

2 Tbsp (30 mL) honey

½ tsp (2 mL) cinnamon

¼ cup (60 mL) toasted pecans, chopped

Topping

2 Tbsp (30 mL) white sugar

¼ tsp (1 mL) cinnamon

¼ cup (60 mL) toasted pecans, chopped

Bread Layer

1 loaf challah (or other soft-crusted white bread), cut into 1-inch (2.5 cm) slices

5 large eggs

1½ cups (375 mL) light cream

1 tsp (5 mL) vanilla

1 Tbsp (15 mL) Grand Marnier (or another liqueur such as Kahlua, Amaretto, etc.)

¼ tsp (1 mL) salt

Serves 8.

Per serving: 554 cals, 31.1 g fat, 14.8 g sat. fat, 214 mg cholesterol, 354 mg sodium, 58.8 g carbs, 9.8 g protein

Peaches and Cream Stuffed French Toast

This recipe may sound fussy but it's actually very easy. You'll soon be inventing your own variations!

Stuffed Toasts

1 medium ripe peach or 8 frozen peach slices

Fruit-Fresh® Produce Protector or 2 Tbsp (30 mL) lemon juice, if using fresh peaches

4 1½-inch (4 cm) thick slices white sandwich bread

⅓ cup (80 mL) spreadable cream cheese, chilled

½ cup (125 mL) toasted, sliced blanched almonds

Batter

3 large eggs, beaten

¾ cup (185 mL) whipping cream

1 Tbsp (15 mL) sugar

½ tsp (2 mL) cinnamon

½ tsp (2 mL) vanilla

1 Tbsp (15 mL) brandy or orange-flavoured brandy (optional)

1 cup (250 mL) vegetable oil for frying

2 Tbsp (30 mL) icing sugar, in a shaker or fine mesh sieve for garnishing

1 bottle of peach syrup, preferably Summerland brand

Serves 4, with 2 halves per person.

Per serving (not including syrup): 565 cals, 26.8 g fat, 9.1 g sat. fat, 73 mg cholesterol, 521 mg sodium, 67 g carbs, 13.6 g protein

Preheat the oven to 250°F (120°C) for keeping cooked French toast warm when frying in batches.

If using a fresh peach, peel and cut into eighths; chop each slice into 4 pieces. Place pieces in a bowl and sprinkle with Fruit-Fresh® or lemon juice, gently tossing to coat. Set aside.

Using a sharp knife, cut the bread slices in half diagonally to create 8 thick triangles. Slice a 3-inch (8 cm) line down the middle of the crustless sides. Push the point of the knife towards the corner of the triangle and move from side to side to make an opening. You now have 8 "pockets" ready for stuffing.

Push a piece of peach into the back corner of each pocket, then add 2 teaspoons (10 mL) of cream cheese followed by 3 more peach pieces and 1 teaspoon (5 mL) almonds on top of another 2 teaspoons (10 mL) cream cheese. Gently press each pocket closed; the cream cheese should help to seal them shut.

In a medium bowl, beat the eggs with the cream, sugar, and flavourings. Preheat a ½ inch (1 cm) of vegetable oil in a large, non-stick skillet on medium-high heat. Just before frying, dip each stuffed toast in the batter, letting any excess run back into the bowl. You want them to be well coated but not saturated.

Fry the first side for 3 to 4 minutes, until golden, and then gently flip over. Cook the other side for 2 to 3 minutes more, until browned. If toasts are browning too quickly, turn down the heat slightly. Continue until all the stuffed toasts are fried; keeping them warm on a plate in the oven until ready to serve.

Warm the peach syrup in the microwave on medium low for 1 to 2 minutes, or heat it in a saucepan on low for about 5 minutes. Sprinkle stuffed toasts with icing sugar and the remaining ¼ cup (60 mL) almonds. Serve with warm peach syrup on the side.

Banana Pecan Loaf

A well-loved classic. Use it for making French toast—fabulous!

Preheat the oven to 350°F (180°C), and liberally oil a large loaf pan.

Combine the dry ingredients in a large bowl, and the wet ingredients, including the banana, in a medium bowl. Make a well in the dry ingredients; add the wet ingredients and mix until just combined. Do not overmix.

Pour the batter into the pan and bake for 50 to 60 minutes, or until a toothpick comes out clean. Cool for 5 minutes; turn the loaf out of the pan to cool completely.

2½ cups (620 mL) flour

2 tsp (10 mL) baking soda

½ tsp (2 mL) cinnamon

1 cup (250 mL) sugar

1 cup (250 mL) pecans, toasted and chopped

2 large eggs, lightly beaten

3 ripe bananas (about 1⅓ cups [330 mL] mashed)

¾ cup plus 1 Tbsp (200 mL) canola oil

2 Tbsp (30 mL) water

1 tsp (5 mL) vanilla

Makes 1 loaf with 14 slices.

Per slice: 344 cals, 19.4 g fat, 1.6 g sat. fat, 30 mg cholesterol, 189 mg sodium, 38.1 g carbs, 4.1 g protein

Lemon Walnut Loaf

One of my personal favourites. Try it with fresh fruit and whipped cream for an easy dessert.

Preheat the oven to 350°F (180°C) and liberally butter a large loaf pan. Sift the first three ingredients together; stir in the walnuts. Set aside.

Using a wooden spoon, cream together the butter and sugar; add the eggs and mix until smooth. Start adding the dry ingredients in thirds, alternating with the milk. Mix until just blended; do not overmix.

Pour the batter into the pan and bake for 1 hour, or until a toothpick comes out clean.

Cool completely on a rack, about 30 to 45 minutes.

Mix the glaze ingredients together and let sit until the sugar is dissolved; pour over the cooled loaf.

Let the loaf sit until the glaze has absorbed and set somewhat before slicing.

Loaf

3 cups (750 mL) flour

½ tsp (2 mL) salt

2 tsp (10 mL) baking powder

1 cup (250 mL) toasted walnuts, chopped

1 cup (250 mL) butter, at room temperature

2 cups (500 mL) sugar

4 large eggs

zest of 2 lemons, minced
(reserve lemons to juice for the glaze)

1 cup (250 mL) milk

Lemon Glaze

¼ cup (60 mL) lemon juice (made from squeezing the 2 lemons zested for the loaf)

¼ cup (60 mL) sugar

Makes 1 loaf with 14 slices.

Per glazed slice: 321 cals, 20.8 g fat, 9.5 g sat. fat, 98 mg cholesterol, 116 mg sodium, 27.3 g carbs, 6.5 g protein

Chocolate Orange Zucchini Loaf

This recipe is the best use for all the extra zucchini you have in the fall. Loaves freeze well too.

Preheat the oven to 350°F (180°C) and butter two large loaf pans. Sift the dry ingredients together; set aside.

In a large bowl, beat the eggs; gradually beat in the sugar until the mixture becomes fluffy and pale ivory in colour. In a large measuring cup or small bowl, combine the zucchini with the buttermilk. Start stirring the flour mixture into the eggs in thirds, alternating with the buttermilk mixture. Add the vanilla, orange zest, and nuts; stir well to incorporate.

Pour the batter into the pans and bake for 30 to 45 minutes. Loaves are done when a toothpick comes out clean.

Cool for 10 minutes while you prepare the glaze.

In a medium-large bowl, whisk together the icing sugar and orange juice until smooth; add the zest and butter and mix well.

Remove the loaves from the pans and glaze while still warm. Let the loaves sit until the glaze has absorbed and set somewhat before slicing.

Loaf

2 cups (500 mL) flour

1 tsp (5 mL) baking soda

1 tsp (5 mL) cinnamon

½ tsp (2 mL) nutmeg

½ cup (125 mL) unsweetened dark Dutch cocoa powder

¼ tsp (1 mL) salt

2 cups (500 mL) sugar

¼ cup (60 mL) vegetable oil

2 cups (500 mL) grated zucchini

¼ cup (60 mL) buttermilk or plain yogurt

1 tsp (5 mL) vanilla

zest of 1 large orange, minced (about 2 Tbsp [30 mL])

1½ cups (375 mL) toasted pecans or walnuts, chopped

Orange Glaze

2 cups (500 mL) sifted icing sugar

3 Tbsp (45 mL) orange juice

2 Tbsp (30 mL) orange zest, minced

2 Tbsp (30 mL) melted butter

Makes 2 loaves with 14 slices each.

Per glazed slice: 206 cals, 7.3 g fat, 1 g sat. fat, 2 mg cholesterol, 114 mg sodium, 32.8 g carbs, 2 g protein

French Breakfast Muffins

These muffins taste a lot like cinnamon sugar donuts!

Preheat the oven to 400°F (200°C) and liberally butter a muffin tin with 6 large cups.

Combine the dry ingredients in a large mixing bowl. In another bowl, whisk together the egg, milk, and melted butter. Add the wet ingredients to the dry ingredients; stir until just mixed. Do not overmix. Portion batter evenly between the 6 muffin cups. Bake for 20 to 25 minutes, or until a toothpick comes out clean.

In a small bowl, mix the sugar, cinnamon, and vanilla. Set topping aside. When the muffins have cooled for 2 to 3 minutes, carefully remove them from the pan. Dip the whole top of each muffin into the melted butter, then into topping mixture. Repeat with each muffin until all the tops are sugar-coated. The sugar mixture will harden slightly and adhere to the muffins once they have cooled completely.

Maple Walnut Variation

Add ¼ cup (60 mL) toasted chopped walnuts to the dry ingredients. Add ¼ teaspoon (1 mL) maple flavouring (preferably Mapleine) to the wet ingredients and ½ teaspoon (2 mL) to the topping.

Butterscotch Pecan Variation

Add ¼ cup (60 mL) chopped toasted pecans to the dry ingredients. Add ½ teaspoon (2 mL) butterscotch flavouring to the wet ingredients and ¼ teaspoon (1 mL) butterscotch flavouring to the topping.

Muffins

1⅔ cups (410 mL) flour

¾ cup (185 mL) sugar

2 tsp (10 mL) baking powder

¼ tsp (1 mL) salt

½ tsp (2 mL) nutmeg

½ cup (125 mL) milk

1 large egg, beaten

⅓ cup (80 mL) melted butter

Topping

1 tsp (5 mL) cinnamon

½ cup (125 mL) sugar

½ tsp (2 mL) vanilla

⅓ cup (80 mL) melted butter, in a small bowl

Makes 6 large muffins.

Per muffin: 505 cals, 22.4 g fat, 13.6 g sat. fat, 93 mg cholesterol, 124 mg sodium, 70.4 g carbs, 5.5 g protein

Per Maple Walnut muffin: 539 cals, 25.5 g fat, 13.9 g sat. fat, 93 mg cholesterol, 124 mg sodium, 71.4 g carbs, 6.2 g protein

Per Butterscotch Pecan muffin: 540 cals, 25.8 g fat, 13.9 g sat. fat, 93 mg cholesterol, 124 mg sodium, 71.4 g carbs, 5.9 g protein

Traditional English Scones

This recipe is a base for the variations that follow but it also makes excellent plain scones. Serve plain ones warm with Honey Almond Spread (p. 19), filled with preserves and whipped cream, or use for egg-filled breakfast sandwiches.

1¾ cups (435 mL) flour

1 tsp (5 mL) baking soda

1½ tsp (2 mL) baking powder

½ tsp (2 mL) salt

¼ cup (60 mL) sugar

¼ cup (60 mL) cold butter

⅔ cup (160 mL) milk

1 large egg

Makes 6 large scones.

Per scone: 263 cals, 9.8 g fat, 5.8 g sat. fat, 60 mg cholesterol, 432 mg sodium, 38.1 g carbs, 5.8 g protein

Per Cranberry Hazelnut scone: 375 cals, 15.9 g fat, 6.2 g sat. fat, 60 mg cholesterol, 434 mg sodium, 50.8 g carbs, 7.4 g protein

Per Cheddar Pecan scone: 424 cals, 23.9 g fat, 10.9 g sat. fat, 83 mg cholesterol, 597 mg sodium, 40.2 g carbs, 12.2 g protein

Preheat the oven to 400°F (200°C) and lightly dust a baking sheet with flour.

In a large mixing bowl, sift the dry ingredients together; cut in the cold butter until it is the size of peas. Set aside. In another bowl, beat the egg and mix in the milk. Make a well in the dry ingredients and pour in the wet ingredients; mix with a fork until just mixed. Do not overmix.

Dust a working surface lightly with flour. Turn out the dough and form it into an 8-inch (20 cm) circle; it will be about 1 inch (2.5 cm) thick. Dust the top with some flour.

Cut into 6 wedges using a flour-coated knife that is wiped clean between each cut. Place scones on a baking sheet, 1 to 2 inches (2.5 to 5 cm) apart. Bake for 8 to 10 minutes, or until their centres spring back when pressed.

Cranberry Hazelnut Variation

After cutting in the butter, add ½ cup (125 mL) dried cranberries, ½ cup (125 mL) chopped toasted blanched hazelnuts, and ½ teaspoon (2 mL) cinnamon to the dry ingredients. Add 1 teaspoon (5 mL) vanilla to the wet ingredients.

Cheddar Pecan Variation

Oil the baking sheet for this variation because the cheese sticks.

After cutting in the butter, add ½ cup (125 mL) toasted chopped pecans and 1 cup (250 mL) grated sharp cheddar cheese to the dry ingredients. Add 1½ tablespoons (22.5 mL) Dijon mustard to the wet ingredients.

Honey Almond Spread

This spread tastes great on toasted bread, bagels, English muffins, and scones.

In a small bowl, mix the honey and almond butter with a spoon until smooth; mix in the cinnamon.

Stored in an airtight container, this spread will keep for 1 week at room temperature.

¼ cup (60 mL) honey

2 Tbsp (30 mL) almond butter

¼ tsp (1 mL) cinnamon

Makes 6 Tbsp (90 mL).

Per Tbsp (15 mL): 81 cals, 3.1 g fat, 0.3 g sat. fat, 1 mg sodium, 12.5 g carbs, 0.8 g protein

Double Chocolate Hazelnut Muffins

These muffins are a special treat for family and friends on the weekend.

Preheat the oven to 400°F (200°C) and liberally butter a muffin tin with 8 large cups.

In a large mixing bowl, combine all the dry ingredients, except the coffee and 2 tablespoons (30 mL) of the hazelnuts. In a separate bowl, beat together the last five ingredients; stir the wet mixture into the dry ingredients until just mixed. Do not overmix.

Portion the batter evenly between 7 muffin cups, filling right to the top; sprinkle the tops with the remaining 2 tablespoons (30 mL) of hazelnuts. Bake for 25 minutes, or until a toothpick comes out clean.

1¾ cups (435 mL) flour

½ cup (125 mL) white sugar

½ cup (125 mL) brown sugar

3 Tbsp (45 mL) unsweetened dark Dutch cocoa powder

1½ tsp (2 mL) baking powder

1½ tsp (2 mL) baking soda

1 tsp (5 mL) salt

½ cup (125 mL) chocolate chips

¼ cup plus 2 Tbsp (90 mL) toasted hazelnuts, chopped

2 large eggs

½ cup (125 mL) canola oil

¾ cup (185 mL) sour cream or plain yogurt

1 tsp (5 mL) vanilla

1 Tbsp (15 mL) instant coffee powder or granules

Makes 7 large muffins.

Per muffin: 553 cals, 26.5 g fat, 5.2 g sat. fat, 62 mg cholesterol, 652 mg sodium, 69.8 g carbs, 8.8 g protein

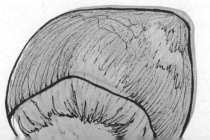

Spiced Carrot Muffins

These muffins taste just like carrot cake!

Preheat the oven to 400°F (200°C) and liberally butter a muffin tin with 9 large cups.

In a medium bowl, mix together the dry ingredients with the nuts. Set aside.

In a large bowl, cream together the butter and sugar; add the egg and vanilla. Beat well and stir in the carrots and raisins. Add the dry ingredients, mixing only until just blended.

Add the applesauce and mix only until just combined.

Portion the batter evenly between the muffin cups, filling right to the top. Bake for 25 to 30 minutes, or until a toothpick comes out clean.

1¾ cups (435 mL) flour

1½ tsp (7.5 mL) cinnamon

1 tsp (5 mL) allspice

1 tsp (5 mL) nutmeg

¼ tsp (1 mL) salt

1 tsp (5 mL) baking soda

½ cup (125 mL) toasted pecans, chopped

½ cup (125 mL) butter

1 cup (250 mL) sugar

1 large egg

1 tsp (5 mL) vanilla

½ cup (125 mL) grated carrot

½ cup (125 mL) raisins

1 cup (250 mL) unsweetened applesauce

Makes 9 large muffins.

Per muffin: 372 cals, 15.6 g fat, 7.1 g sat. fat, 51 mg cholesterol, 217 mg sodium, 53.8 g carbs, 4.2 g protein

Almond Cranberry Granola

This cereal is great sprinkled on some fruit for breakfast or as a healthy snack.

4½ cups (1125 mL) large-flake oats, preferably Robin Hood or Quaker

2¼ cups (560 mL) whole almonds, raw or blanched

¾ tsp (4 mL) cinnamon

⅔ cup (160mL) honey, preferably in a glass measuring cup

¼ cup (60 mL) vegetable oil

1 tsp (5 mL) vanilla

¾ cup (185 mL) dried cranberries, added after baking and cooling

Makes 8 cups (2 L).

Per ½ cup (125 mL): 403 calories, 17.1 g fat, 1.7 g sat. fat, 4 mg sodium, 50.4 g carbs, 11.8 g protein

Preheat the oven to 350°F (180°C). Line two baking sheets with foil and oil them well (or use parchment paper, which doesn't need to be oiled).

Mix the oats, almonds, and cinnamon in a large bowl. Heat the honey in the microwave for 30 to 60 seconds on low to liquefy it. Mix the oil and the vanilla with the honey; pour it into the oat mixture and stir to coat thoroughly. Spoon the mixture onto the two baking sheets and spread it out evenly.

Bake for 10 minutes; stir well and spread out the mixture evenly again. The stirring is essential because the edges will brown quicker than the middle. Bake for another 10 to 15 minutes, until completely golden.

Cool the granola before adding the cranberries. Store in an airtight container for up to 1 week, or freeze for up to 3 months.

Soups and Sandwiches

Curried Chicken Soup
with Peanuts and Lime

If you prefer a rich, creamy soup, substitute 1 can of coconut milk for 1¾ cups (435 mL) of stock.

Heat the stock in a large saucepan on medium-high heat; add the carrots, onions, and celery. Cook at a low boil until the vegetables are tender, about 15 minutes. Frequently skim off any froth that forms and discard it.

Add the seasonings, lime juice, sugar, and chicken; reduce the heat to low. Simmer the soup for 5 to 10 minutes to heat through, stirring occasionally. Add the rice and cooked vegetables; simmer 5 to 10 minutes more to heat them.

Ladle the soup into bowls; sprinkle each serving with ¼ tablespoons (4 mL) cilantro and 2 tablespoons (30 mL) peanuts.

6 cups (1.5 L) chicken stock

½ cup (125 mL) diced carrots

½ cup (125 mL) diced onion
(about half a medium onion)

⅓ cup (80 mL) diced celery

½ tsp (2 mL) Thai red curry paste

½ tsp (2 mL) ground lemon grass
or 1 Tbsp (15 mL) fresh lemon grass
(white tip area only), minced

½ tsp (2 mL) curry powder

½ tsp (2 mL) salt

½ tsp (2 mL) freshly ground pepper

1 Tbsp plus 1 tsp (20 mL) lime juice

1 tsp (5 mL) sugar

1½ cups (375 mL) cooked,
coarsely chopped chicken

1 cup (250 mL) cooked long-grain white rice

1 cup (250 mL) chopped, cooked
green vegetables, such as beans,
broccoli, zucchini, or peas

1 Tbsp (15 mL) minced cilantro leaves

½ cup (125 mL) roasted
unsalted peanuts, chopped

Serves 4.

Per 1½ cups (375 mL): 326 cals, 12.8 g fat,
2.2 g sat. fat, 42 mg cholesterol, 1531 mg sodium,
22.2 g carbs, 30.5 g protein

Almond Bisque with Chicken and Leeks

Makes a hearty, comforting lunch for a rainy day (or any day).

In a large saucepan, heat the soup base on medium-low, stirring frequently.

Add the chicken and rice; cook for 5 to 10 minutes until heated through.

In a small bowl, whisk the nut butter with ½ cup (125 mL) of warm soup base, taken from the pot, until smooth. Add this mixture to the soup and stir well to combine.

Ladle the soup into bowls, garnishing each one with 2 to 3 teaspoons (10 to 15 mL) of the toasted almonds.

1 large leek (white and light green parts only), diced and washed

1 recipe Cream Soup Base (p. 26), (substituting diced leek for the onion), at room temperature

3 Tbsp (45 mL) almond butter

2 cups (500 mL) cooked chicken (about 14 oz [435 g]), cut into bite-sized cubes

1½ cups (375 mL) cooked long-grain white rice (or use peeled and cubed cooked potatoes)

½ cup (125 mL) toasted sliced, blanched almonds

Serves 8.

Per 1 ⅛ cups (280 mL): 362 cals, 20.9 g fat, 8 g sat. fat, 68 mg cholesterol, 481 mg sodium, 27.4 g carbs, 16.3 g protein

Cream Soup Base

This all-purpose cream soup base can be used for any soup containing vegetables, fish, seafood, or meat. I use stock instead of water if the soup ingredients are mild in flavour.

4 cups (1 L) water or stock, depending on preference

½ cup (125 mL) diced onion (about half a medium onion)

2 cups (500 mL) whipping cream

1 tsp (5 mL) salt

½ tsp (2 mL) garlic salt

½ tsp (2 mL) pepper

2 Tbsp (30 mL) minced fresh parsley leaves or dried parsley

1 cup (250 mL) flour

Makes 8 cups (2 L).

Per cup (250 mL): 164 cals, 11.3 g fat, 6.9 g sat. fat, 41 mg cholesterol, 454 mg sodium, 13.8 g carbs, 2.3 g protein

Cooking Tip:

If you are adding grated cheese to the base it will take 2 cups (500 mL) to flavour 8 cups (2 L) of base. Sharp or aged cheddar, Edam, or Monterey Jack all work well with vegetable (broccoli, cauliflower or potato), meat (sausage or chicken), or shellfish (shrimp, crab, lobster, or chowder) soups. Heat the soup base on medium-low heat, then add the cheese, and stir until melted and smooth.

In a large saucepan or stockpot, bring 1 cup (250 mL) of water/stock to a boil.

Add the onions and cover the pot. Turn the heat down and cook onions on medium heat for 6 to 8 minutes, until transparent; stir occasionally. Add the cream and the seasoning; mix well and cook for 5 to 10 minutes to heat through.

In a medium bowl, whisk the flour with 2 cups (500 mL) of water/stock until smooth. When adding the flour mixture, the soup should be hot but not boiling. (If it starts boiling, remove the pot from the burner briefly until it stops.)

Strain the flour mix into the pot through a sieve, stirring the base constantly to prevent lumps from forming. Turn down the heat to medium-low; cook until base thickens, stirring constantly. This will take about 5 minutes. Add the remaining 1 cup (250 mL) of water/stock to the base all at once and stir until smooth.

Cover the soup base while it cools to prevent a skin from forming on the surface. Refrigerate, covered, for up to 3 days. The soup base can be frozen for up to 3 months. To reheat, thaw first and then heat in a saucepan on medium-low heat, whisking frequently, for 8 to 10 minutes.

Roasted Red Pepper Soup with Orzo and Feta

This soup has a lively colour and a robust flavour!

Purée the peppers and the walnuts in a food processor or blender until smooth, adding ¼ to ½ cup (60 to 125 mL) of the soup water if needed. Set aside.

In a medium-large saucepan or stockpot, cook the shallots in ½ cup (125 mL) water on medium heat. Add the whipping cream and another ½ cup (125 mL) of water; heat the mixture to steaming but not boiling. (If it starts boiling, remove the pot from the burner briefly until it stops.)

In a medium bowl, whisk the flour with the remaining water. Strain the flour mix into the pot through a sieve, stirring constantly because the soup will thicken quickly. Once the soup has thickened, reduce the heat to low.

Whisk in the seasoning; add the pepper–walnut purée and the pasta. Simmer for 5 to 10 minutes to heat through.

In a small bowl, mix together the feta cheese, walnuts, and parsley. Ladle the soup into bowls and sprinkle each one with a spoonful of the topping.

Cooking tip:

Before making this recipe, toast ½ cup (125 mL) walnuts so you have enough for the soup and the topping.

Soup

½ cup (125 mL) packed, chopped roasted red peppers

¼ cup (60 mL) toasted walnuts, chopped

2 shallots, minced (about ¼ cup [60 mL])

2 cups (500 mL) water

1 cup (250 mL) whipping cream

½ cup (125 mL) flour

½ tsp (2 mL) salt

¼ tsp (1 mL) garlic salt

½ tsp (2 mL) pepper

1½ cups (375 mL) cooked orzo or another small pasta, or cooked long-gram white rice

Topping

½ cup (125 mL) feta cheese, rinsed, patted dry, and crumbled

¼ cup (60 mL) toasted walnuts, chopped

2 Tbsp (30 mL) fresh parsley leaves, minced

Serves 4.

Per 1¼ cups (310 mL) with topping: 497 cals, 34.8 g fat, 16.7 g sat. fat, 95 mg cholesterol, 624 mg sodium, 35.2 g carbs, 10.8 g protein

Sherry Spiked Mushroom and Chestnut Soup

This soup combines chestnuts and mushrooms with coconut milk for a rich soup with a very subtle flavour. It is great as a first course for a special dinner, or pair it with a salad for an elegant lunch.

1 Tbsp (15 mL) butter

¼ cup (60 mL) diced onion (about half a small onion)

½ lb (250 g) white mushrooms, sliced and coarsely chopped

¼ cup (60 mL) dry white wine

1 tsp (5 mL) lemon juice

2 cups (500 mL) chicken stock (or substitute vegetable stock for a vegetarian soup)

¼ tsp (1 mL) garlic salt

1 tsp (5 mL) salt

¼ tsp (1 mL) pepper

¼ tsp (1 mL) Tabasco sauce

⅛ tsp (0.5 mL) ground nutmeg

1 Tbsp (15 mL) dried parsley

1 14-oz (398 mL) can coconut milk, shaken well before opening

2 Tbsp (30 mL) smooth, unsweetened chestnut purée

½ cup (125 mL) flour

1 Tbsp (15 mL) dry sherry

Serves 4.

Per cup: 273 cals, 17.8 g fat, 13.2 g sat. fat, 9 mg cholesterol, 1152 mg sodium, 21.3 g carbs, 7 g protein

In a medium saucepan, melt the butter on medium-high heat; add the onions, wine, and lemon juice. Cook covered, stirring occasionally, for 4 to 5 minutes, until the onions are transparent.

Add the mushrooms and cook covered for 4 to 5 minutes to sweat them before taking off the lid and continuing to cook them until almost dry. This will take 5 to 7 minutes.

When the mushrooms start to brown slightly, add 1 cup (250 mL) of the stock and reduce the heat to medium. Stir the mixture to release any brown juice from the bottom of the pan and add seasonings.

Whisk the chestnut purée with ⅓ cup (80 mL) water until smooth, pressing through a sieve if necessary to remove any lumps. Add the thinned chestnut purée and coconut milk to the soup; mix well to incorporate.

In a medium-sized bowl, whisk the flour with the remaining 1 cup (250 mL) of stock. The soup should be hot but not boiling when adding the flour mixture. If it starts boiling, remove from the heat until it stops.

Strain the flour mix into the pot through a sieve, stirring constantly until it thickens.

Turn the heat down to low, cover the pot, and simmer for 20 to 30 minutes, stirring occasionally.

Tuscan Tomato Soup

An easy, quick soup made from common pantry items but which tastes like you used fresh tomatoes.

In a large saucepan or stockpot, heat the olive oil on medium. Add the onions and cook, covered, for 5 minutes, until transparent. Uncover and add the wine and sherry; boil until half the liquid evaporates, which should take 7 to 10 minutes.

Add the garlic, sugar, parsley, and the stock; continue boiling for another 8 to 10 minutes, until the volume reduces to ½ to ¾ cup (125 to 185 mL).

Add the V8 juice and the salt and pepper; reduce the heat to medium-low. In a food processor, pulse the diced tomatoes 5 to 6 times, or process them on medium-high for 5 to 6 seconds instead; you want a coarse purée. Add the tomato purée to the soup and cook for 5 to 10 minutes. Reduce the heat to low and cook for 20 minutes more, stirring occasionally.

In a medium bowl, stir together the cheese and the pesto until combined. Ladle the soup into bowls, topping each one with 3 tablespoons (45 mL) of pesto cheese and, if desired, ¼ cup (60 mL) of croutons.

Italian Tomato Bread Soup Variation
Increase the amount of croutons per serving to 1 cup (250 mL).

Soup

¼ cup (60 mL) olive oil

1 cup (250 mL) diced onion (one medium onion)

½ cup (125 mL) dry wine, red or white

2 Tbsp (30 mL) sherry vinegar (or balsamic vinegar)

½ tsp (2 mL) minced garlic

2 Tbsp (30 mL) sugar

2 Tbsp (30 mL) dried parsley

1 cup (250 mL) chicken stock

2 5-oz (156 mL) cans (or 1 14-oz [340mL] can) V8 juice

¾ tsp (4 mL) salt

½ tsp (2 mL) pepper

2 28-oz (796 mL) cans diced tomatoes with juice

Topping

1½ cups (375 mL) grated Edam or Monterey Jack cheese, at room temperature

3 Tbsp (45 mL) Basil Pesto (p. 94) or substitute purchased pesto, at room temperature

1½ cups (375 mL) Herb Croutons (p. 30) or purchased ones, at room temperature (optional)

Serves 6.

Per 1½ cup (375 mL) serving: 319 cals, 20.8 g fat, 6.3 g sat. fat, 20 mg cholesterol, 1191 mg sodium, 21.5 g carbs, 11.5 g protein

Herb Croutons

This recipe is not an exact science; the measurements are estimates. Season and oil the croutons sufficiently or they won't be very tasty. If seasoned well, they make a great snack; they taste just like garlic toast!

2 cups (500 mL) 1-inch (2.5 cm) white bread cubes, made from a French baguette or an Italian loaf

⅓ cup (80 mL) olive oil, preferably in a bottle with a pour spout

¼ tsp (1 mL) garlic salt in a shaker

¼ tsp (1 mL) pepper in a shaker or grinder

½ tsp (2 mL) dried oregano, loose or in a shaker

Makes 2 cups (500 mL).

Per ¼ cup (60 mL) (about 8 croutons): 132 cals, 9.2 g fat, 1.2 g sat. fat, 216 mg sodium, 10.8 g carbs, 1.4 g protein

Preheat the oven to 375°F (190°C).

Place the bread cubes in a medium bowl and drizzle them with 2 tablespoons (30 mL) of the oil. Stir them up and drizzle with another 2 tablespoons (30 mL) of oil before stirring again. The idea is to coat them evenly with oil so the seasoning will stick. Drizzle with the remaining oil and stir once more. Sprinkle the cubes evenly with half of each seasoning. Stir them up again and sprinkle them again with the rest of each seasoning.

Bake the seasoned bread cubes on a baking sheet for 10 minutes. Remove from the oven and stir again before returning to the oven for another 5 to 8 minutes, baking until golden brown.

Cool croutons completely on a rack, and then store in an airtight container for 3 to 4 days or freeze them for up to 1 month.

Italian Garden Sandwiches

These are great as a traditional sandwich on fresh bread but can also be grilled.

Drain the sun-dried tomatoes and blot them dry with a paper towel.

In a small bowl, mix the cream cheese with the pesto until combined. (This step can also be done in a mini chopper or food processor.) Spread each bread slice with 1 tablespoon (15 mL) of pesto spread.

Divide the tomato and artichoke pieces evenly amongst the cheese-covered bread slices, and then layer with the lettuce before closing the sandwich. Gently press down on the top of the sandwich when you cut it in two to hold it together.

4 medium sun-dried tomatoes, chopped into ¼-inch (6 mm) pieces and soaked in hot water for 15 minutes

1 14-oz (398 mL) can artichoke hearts, rinsed, dried off, and sliced ¼ inch (6 mm) thick

1 4-oz (113 g) package regular cream cheese, at room temperature

2 Tbsp (30 mL) Basil Pesto (p. 94)

8 slices of your favourite sandwich bread

green-leaf lettuce leaves

Serves 4.

Per sandwich: 504 cals, 19.7 g fat, 10.3 g sat. fat, 83 g cholesterol, 749 g sodium, 67.1 g carbs, 14.8 g protein

Mediterranean Beef Sandwiches

Substantial but rich and rewarding at the same time!

2 Tbsp (30 mL) butter

1 medium onion, peeled,
cut in half, and sliced thin

8 ½-inch (1 cm) thick crusty French
baguette slices, 3- × 4-inch (8 × 10 cm) size

½ cup (125 mL) Mediterranean
Walnut Spread (p. 37)

10 oz (300 g) roast beef or steak, sliced thin

4 slices of Edam, Swiss, or Havarti
cheese, cut in half to fit bread slices

Serves 4, with 2 open-faced sandwich slices per person.

Per sandwich slice: 240 cals, 13.1 g fat, 4.6 g sat. fat, 49 mg
cholesterol, 342 mg sodium, 14.6 g carbs, 16 g protein

Melt the butter in a medium, non-stick skillet on medium-high heat. Add the onions and cook, covered, for 2 to 3 minutes to sweat them. Uncover and continue to cook, stirring frequently, until the onions turn golden brown, about 5 to 8 minutes. Remove from heat and let cool.

Preheat the broiler, oil a baking sheet with sides, and position a rack in the top third of the oven.

Spread each slice of baguette with 1 tablespoon (15 mL) of Mediterranean Walnut Spread. Top each slice with an eighth of the beef, 1 tablespoon (15 mL) onions, and half a cheese slice.

Broil the sandwiches until the cheese is melted and they are golden brown on top, about 4 to 6 minutes. Serve immediately.

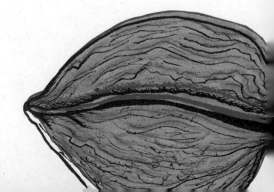

Dijon Chicken Salad Croissants

A great picnic or weekend lunch idea.

Spread croissants with 1½ teaspoons (7.5 mL) of butter per side. (While this step is optional, I find croissants can become a little soggy without the butter if they sit for a while.)

Spread ⅔ cup (160 mL) of chicken salad evenly on the bottom halves of the croissants, and top each one with 2 tomato slices and a piece of lettuce. If desired, cut croissants in two to serve.

6 plain croissants, sliced in half

⅓ cup (80 mL) butter, at room temperature (optional)

1 recipe Dijon Chicken Salad with Cucumber and Cashews (p. 69)

12 small tomato slices (2 medium tomatoes, sliced)

6 small leaves green-leaf lettuce, or 3 larger leaves ripped in two

Serves 6.

Per croissant: 742 cals, 56.1 g fat, 17.1 g sat. fat, 115 mg cholesterol, 1029 mg sodium, 38 g carbs, 21.2 g protein

Shrimp and Cashew Wraps

I prefer Olafson's flour tortillas for making wraps because they are flavourful and roll easily.

6 10-inch (25 cm) plain flour tortillas

1 recipe Cashew Cream Cheese Spread (p. 34), at room temperature

1½ cups (375 mL) cooked shrimp meat, rinsed and patted dry

⅔ cup (160 mL) diced English cucumber (about one third of a large cucumber)

⅔ cup (160 mL) diced fresh tomato (about one medium tomato)

6 medium romaine lettuce leaves, shredded thin

¾ cup (185 mL) salsa (not fresh cut), or Avocado Sauce (p. 49)

Serves 6.

Per wrap: 439 cals, 26.7 g fat, 12.5 g sat. fat, 103 mg cholesterol, 915 mg sodium, 32.4 g carbs, 17.1 g protein

Working with 1 or 2 tortillas at a time, spread each one with ¼ cup (60 mL) of Cashew Cream Cheese, leaving bare 2 inches (5 cm) of the edge closest to you.

Place a sixth of the shredded lettuce along the lower third of each tortilla, on top of the cream cheese spread. Top each lettuce row with ¼ cup (60 mL) shrimp and 2 tablespoons (30 mL) each of tomatoes and cucumber. Spoon 2 tablespoons (30 mL) of salsa or Avocado Sauce along the row.

Fold the tortilla edge without any cheese over the fillings and roll it up tightly. Place seam side down in a covered container and refrigerate for 20 to 30 minutes to help seal in the fillings. Continue until all the wraps are rolled and chilled. Slice each wrap in half on the diagonal; serve with halves propped up on each other to show off the filling.

Cashew Cream Cheese Spread

Great for wraps and vegetarian sandwiches, or serve with crackers and fresh veggies. This spread can be made 1 to 2 days ahead.

8 oz (250 g) regular cream cheese, at room temperature

1 Tbsp (15 mL) lime juice, at room temperature

½ tsp (2 mL) garlic salt

½ tsp (2 mL) pepper

1 Tbsp (15 mL) minced fresh cilantro

½ cup (125 mL) toasted cashews, chopped

Makes 1½ cups (375 mL).

Per Tbsp (15 mL): 62 cals, 5.6 g fat, 2.8 g sat. fat, 12 mg cholesterol, 94 mg sodium, 1.5 g carbs, 1.4 g protein

In a medium bowl, mix the cream cheese together with the lime juice, garlic salt, and pepper. Add the cilantro and nuts; stir to combine well. Cover and refrigerate if not using right away. (Bring to room temperature for easy spreading.)

small Bites

Baked Mushroom and Almond Dip

This is an excellent party recipe because it makes enough for about 15 people and can be easily doubled to serve a larger group.

Dip
Heat the oil in a large, non-stick skillet on medium-high. Add the mushrooms, cover, and sweat them for 2 to 3 minutes to release the water. Add the lemon juice and garlic; cook uncovered until the mushrooms are almost dry, about 5 minutes. Stir them occasionally to cook them evenly and prevent sticking. Remove from heat and cool to room temperature, about 20 minutes. In a large bowl, whisk together the cream cheese, mayonnaise, herbs and seasoning. Add the green onions, almonds, and cooled mushroom mixture; stir well to combine.

Bread Bowl
Cut a slice 1 to 1½ inches (2.5 to 4 cm) thick off the top of the loaf, and reserve it for later use as a lid.

Pull out the soft inside bread to make a bowl to hold the dip; leaving a 1-inch (2.5 cm) thick shell. (The inside bread can be used for breadcrumbs, or cubed and frozen for croutons or stuffing.)

Fill the bread bowl to the brim with dip and replace the crusty lid. Wrap well in aluminum foil. (You can prepare the dip to this point up to 1 day ahead. Keep refrigerated and bring the dip to room temperature before baking.)

Baking and Serving
Preheat the oven to 350°F (180°C) with a rack in the middle of the oven. Bake the dip for 90 minutes. To serve, unwrap the aluminum foil, remove the lid, and platter the loaf. Serve with baguette slices and/or crackers on the side, and a spreader knife or two.

Dip
2 tsp (10 mL) vegetable oil

¾ lb (375 g) mushrooms, chopped into ¼-inch (6 mm) pieces

1 Tbsp (15 mL) lemon juice

½ tsp (2 mL) minced garlic

1 lb (500 g) regular cream cheese, at room temperature

1 cup (250 mL) mayonnaise, preferably Hellmann's or Kraft Real Mayonnaise

1 tsp (5 mL) salt

½ tsp (2 mL) cayenne pepper

1 Tbsp (15 mL) dried parsley or 2 Tbsp (30 mL) minced fresh parsley leaves

1 bunch green onions (about 6), trimmed and finely chopped

½ cup (125 mL) toasted blanched almonds, finely chopped

Bread Bowl
1 large round loaf Italian or sourdough bread, about 8 inches (20 cm) across

aluminum foil for wrapping the dip-filled bread loaf

sliced French baguette and/or crackers to serve with dip

Makes 3½ cups (875 mL) of dip.

Per ¼ cup (60 mL) dip: 231 cals, 20.3 g fat, 8.3 g sat. fat, 40 mg cholesterol, 385 mg sodium, 7.6 g carbs, 4.3 g protein

Mediterranean Walnut Spread
with Warm Pita Wedges

If you have a food processor, this is an easy-to-make vegetarian/ vegan spread that can be prepared 1 to 2 days ahead. Pita bread is the traditional choice with Mediterranean snacks but this spread is also great when served with sliced baguette or crackers.

Add all ingredients to the food processor bowl, except the parsley and olives. Purée continuously until smooth, stopping to scrape down the sides of the bowl several times during the purée process. Stir in the olive pieces and 3½ tablespoons (52.5 mL) parsley. Place into a serving bowl and refrigerate unless serving immediately.

Lightly oil both sides of each pita bread and grill on a barbecue (preheated to 400°F [200°C]), or fry in a medium skillet on medium-high heat until light golden, about 1 to 2 minutes per side. Cut each piece into 8 wedges.

Garnish the dip with the remaining parsley and present with pita wedges on the side. If you make the dip ahead, bring it to room temperature before serving.

1½ cups (375 mL) toasted walnut pieces

2 roasted red peppers, peeled and chopped (about 1 cup [250 mL])

½ cup (125 mL) breadcrumbs, preferably fresh

⅓ cup (80 mL) ketchup

1 tsp (5 mL) cumin

½ tsp (2 mL) allspice

½ to 1 tsp (2.5 to 5 mL) chili pepper flakes (1 tsp [5 mL] gives the spread a mildly hot taste)

¼ cup (60 mL) olive oil

½ tsp (2 mL) salt

¼ tsp (1 mL) pepper

½ cup (125 mL) coarsely chopped black olives, rinsed and well drained

¼ cup (60 mL) minced fresh parsley

1 package of pita bread containing 5 pitas

olive oil or other vegetable oil for frying

Makes 2½ cups (625 mL) of spread.

Per ¼ cup (60 mL) spread with 4 pita wedges: 301 cals, 18.3 g fat, 2 g sat. fat, 570 mg sodium, 27.6 g carbs, 6.4 g protein

Caponata

There is a lot of dicing required to prepare this appetizer but it is well worth it! Italians would choose crusty bread to accompany this tasty topping but toasted pita wedges or crackers are also suitable.

Heat the olive oil in a large non-stick skillet on medium-high heat. Add the onions, peppers, and eggplant and cook until golden and soft, about 15 minutes. Stir the mixture frequently while cooking. Add the garlic in the last 5 minutes of the cooking time.

Turn the heat down to medium and add the tomatoes, capers, vinegar, sugar, and seasoning. Cover and simmer for 4 to 5 minutes to blend the flavours.

Remove from heat and mix in the basil and pine nuts. To serve, present the warm caponata in a bowl surrounded by fresh baguette slices.

2 Tbsp (30 mL) olive oil

1 medium onion, cut into ½-inch (1 cm) cubes

1 yellow pepper, seeded and cut into ½-inch (1 cm) cubes

1 large eggplant, peeled and cut into ½-inch (1 cm) cubes

1 tsp (5 mL) minced garlic

2 medium-large firm beefsteak tomatoes, peeled and cut into ½-inch (1 cm) cubes

1 Tbsp (15 mL) capers, finely chopped

1 Tbsp plus 1½ tsp (22.5 mL) red wine vinegar or sherry vinegar

½ tsp (2 mL) salt

¼ tsp (1 mL) pepper

½ tsp (2 mL) sugar

¼ cup (60 mL) fresh basil, finely chopped

⅓ cup (80 mL) toasted pine nuts

1 crusty French baguette

Makes approximately 2½ cups (625 mL).

Per 5 Tbsp (75 mL) serving: 93 cals, 6.4 g fat, 0.9 g sat. fat, 183 mg sodium, 6.9 g carbs, 2.2 g protein

Chili Nut Glazed Brie

A sweet and spicy choice for all you cheese lovers!

Preheat the oven to 200°F (90°C) and lightly oil a small baking dish (or use a cheese baker). Carefully slice the rind off the top of the Brie. Cover and bake the cheese for 15 minutes to soften.

Whisk together the brandy, lemon juice, honey, and cayenne, and then add the nuts. Remove the Brie from the oven and pour the glaze overtop.

Bake uncovered for another 10 minutes. Serve the glazed cheese with baguette slices or crackers for dipping.

Cheese Bakers

Cheese bakers designed for 8-inch (20 cm) wheels of cheese are available at many kitchen and department stores. They are usually ceramic or stainless steel, come with a lid, and can be used for both baking and serving cheese.

1 8-oz (250 g) wheel of Brie cheese
1½ tsp (7.5 mL) brandy
1½ tsp (7.5 mL) lemon juice
3 Tbsp (45 mL) honey
⅛ tsp (0.5 mL) cayenne pepper
¼ cup (60 mL) toasted pecans, walnuts, or blanched almonds, coarsely chopped

Serves 6.

Per serving: 196 cals, 13.9 g fat, 6.9 g sat. fat, 38 mg cholesterol, 238 mg sodium, 9.9 g carbs, 8.2 g protein

Cheddar Pecan Chips

These very rich and tasty chips go well with any of the sour cream–based dips that follow.

Oil a large, non-stick skillet and line a baking sheet with parchment paper or greased foil.

Toss all the ingredients together in a medium bowl. Heat the skillet on medium and add 1 tablespoon (15 mL) quantities to the pan, placed 4 inches (10 cm) apart. If the cheese mixture is piled up, flatten slightly to form a 2-inch (5 cm) circle. Cook until they bubble up all over and the undersides turn golden. Using a heat-proof spatula or lifter, gently turn them over and brown the other side.

Cool on parchment or foil, and then move to paper towels to absorb excess oil. Repeat until all the chips are cooked, stirring the cheese mixture between each round. Chips can be made 1 to 2 days ahead of time and are best stored in an airtight container to prevent breakage.

Parmesan Almond Variation
Follow the same technique as for Cheddar Pecan Chips.

1½ cups (375 mL) grated aged or sharp cheddar cheese (about 6 oz [175 g])

¼ cup (60 mL) finely chopped raw pecans

¼ tsp (1 mL) cayenne pepper

Makes about 28 chips.

Per chip: 169 cals, 14.3 g fat, 7.3 g sat. fat, 34 mg cholesterol, 205 g sodium, 1.3 g carbs, 8.6 g protein

Parmesan Almond

2 cups (500 mL) grated Parmesan cheese

¼ cup (60 mL) finely chopped raw almonds, natural or blanched

¼ cup (60 mL) flour

Makes about 28 chips.

Per chip: 44 cals, 2.8 g fat, 1.5 g sat. fat, 6 mg cholesterol, 133 mg sodium, 1.4 g carbs, 3.4 g protein

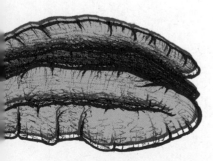

Roasted Red Pepper Dip

The nutritional information for this dip, and the two others that follow, are based on regular sour cream but you can substitute light sour cream with satisfactory results. Fat-free sour cream is a little watery compared to the others and therefore changes the dip consistency.

Whisk all the ingredients together.

    Cover and refrigerate until needed; can be prepared 2 to 3 days ahead. Can be served chilled or at room temperature.

1 cup (250 mL) sour cream
¼ cup (60 mL) puréed roasted red peppers
½ tsp (2 mL) garlic salt
½ tsp (2 mL) pepper

Makes 1¼ cups (310 mL).

Per Tbsp (15 mL): 8 cals, 0.8 g fat, 0.5 g sat fat, 2 mg cholesterol, 26 mg sodium, 0.2 g carbs, 0.1 g protein

Lemon Pepper Dip

Whisk all the ingredients together.

    Cover and refrigerate for 2 to 3 hours to blend the flavours and thicken up the dip.

1 cup (250 mL) sour cream
zest of one lemon, minced
1 Tbsp (15 mL) lemon juice
½ tsp (2 mL) garlic salt
½ tsp (2 mL) freshly ground black pepper

Makes just over 1 cup (250 mL).

Per tsp (4 mL): 10 cals, 0.9 g fat, 0.6 g sat. fat, 2 mg cholesterol, 25 mg sodium, 0.2 g carbs, 0.1 g protein

Cilantro Sour Cream

This sauce goes well with spicy foods, especially Mexican or Indian appetizers.

Whisk the sour cream, cilantro, lime juice, garlic salt, and pepper.

Refrigerate for 1 to 2 hours so the flavours blend and the sour cream regains its thickness.

1 cup (250 mL) sour cream
2 Tbsp (30 mL) minced fresh cilantro leaves
1½ tsp (7.5 mL) lime juice
½ tsp (2 mL) garlic salt
½ tsp (2 mL) pepper

Makes 1 cup (250 mL).

Per 2 tsp (10 mL) serving: 19 cals, 1.8 g fat, 1.1 g sat. fat, 4 mg cholesterol, 49 mg sodium, 0.4 g carbs, 0.3 g protein

Hazelnut Portobello Strips

With their crispy coating, these mushroom appetizers are unique and very delicious when served with a savoury dip.

In a medium bowl, mix the flour with the salt and pepper. In a second medium bowl, whisk one egg to start. In a third medium bowl, mix the nuts with the Panko breadcrumbs.

Dredge the mushroom strips with the flour, shaking off any excess. One at a time, dip each strip in the egg, dripping off any excess before coating well with breadcrumbs. (Whisk a second egg if you are running short of beaten egg to coat them.)

Refrigerate the strips, uncovered, on a plate, for 1 to 2 hours to adhere the coating. They can be made to this point ahead of time, and then brought to room temperature prior to frying.

Preheat the oven to 250°F (120°F) to keep mushroom strips warm while frying in batches. Heat ½ inch (1 cm) of oil in a large non-stick skillet on medium-high heat until the oil starts rippling.

Cook the strips in batches, careful that they don't overlap, until golden on the bottom, about 2 to 3 minutes. Turn them and brown the other side for 1 to 2 minutes.

Place cooked strips onto paper towels to absorb the excess oil. If not serving strips immediately, keep them warm on a baking sheet in the oven.

Serve the warm mushroom strips with a bowl of Roasted Red Pepper Dip.

½ cup (125 mL) flour

¼ tsp (1 mL) salt

¼ tsp (1 mL) pepper

1 to 2 large eggs

¾ cup (185 mL) Panko breadcrumbs

¾ cup (185 mL) toasted blanched hazelnuts, finely chopped

4 large Portobello mushroom caps, sliced into ½-inch (1 cm) thick strips (about 6 per cap)

1 cup (250 mL) canola or corn oil for deep frying

1 recipe Roasted Red Pepper Dip (p. 41)

Makes 24 pieces.

Per piece: 63 cals, 3.9 g fat, 0.4 g sat. fat, 13 mg cholesterol, 58 mg sodium, 5.3 g carbs, 1.8 g protein

Spaghetti Squash Fritters

These fritters make delicate, delicious little appetizers! Use only mild salsa to complement them but not overpower them. This recipe is an excellent way to use up leftover cooked potatoes.

1 cup (250 mL) cooked spaghetti squash

1 medium-large russet potato, peeled, cooked, and grated once cool (about 1 cup [250 mL])

2 Tbsp (30 mL) minced green onion (about 1½)

½ tsp (2 mL) pepper

½ tsp (2 mL) salt

1 Tbsp (15 mL) dried parsley

¼ cup (60 mL) toasted walnuts, finely chopped

2 Tbsp (30 mL) flour

1 large egg, beaten

½ cup (125 mL) canola or corn oil for frying

mild salsa and Cilantro Sour Cream (p. 42) or plain sour cream, if desired

Makes 24 fritters.

Per fritter (without condiments): 31 cals, 2.1 g fat, 0.3 g sat. fat, 9 mg cholesterol, 68 mg sodium, 2.4 g carbs, 0.7 g protein

Preheat the oven to 250°F (120°C) to keep the fried fritters warm until serving.

In a medium-large bowl, mix together the squash, potato, onion, seasoning, parsley, nuts, and flour. Add the egg and mix well.

Heat the oil in a large, non-stick skillet on medium-high heat. When the oil starts rippling, spoon 1 tablespoon (15 mL) portions into the skillet, 2 inches (5 cm) apart, and then flatten the tops with the spoon. Fry the fritters until golden, about 1½ to 2 minutes, and then flip over and cook until the flipped side is browned, about 1 to 2 minutes. You will likely need to cook them in several batches.

Place cooked fritters on a paper towel–lined baking sheet to drain; keep them warm in the oven until ready to serve. Serve warm with salsa and sour cream on the side, if desired.

How to cook spaghetti squash

Preheat the oven to 350°F (180°C).

Use a large knife to split the squash in two from stem to end. Remove the seeds and stringy centre and discard. Place squash halves cut side down in a 1- to 2-inch (2.5 to 5 cm) deep baking dish. Add ½ cup (125 mL) of water.

Bake in the bottom third of the oven for 20 minutes. Check for doneness by scraping at the insides with a dinner fork. Squash is ready when the flesh easily pulls off in thin spaghetti-like strands. If it is not done yet, bake for another 10 minutes and try again.

Once cool, use a fork to remove the cooked flesh from each squash half until only a ¼ inch (6 mm) layer remains, and then switch to a spoon.

The squash can be cooked and shredded a day or two ahead, and frozen spaghetti squash flesh lasts for 3 months if wrapped well. Reheat thawed squash in a covered dish in the microwave on medium high, 2 minutes for 1 cup (250 mL) of squash (no need to add water).

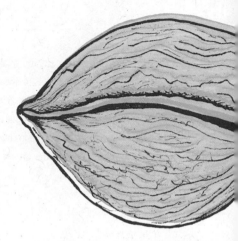

Mango and Pecan Quesadillas

Your family and friends will comment, "These are great!" and then ask, "What's in these?" While you are working, keep the tortillas in a plastic bag, or their original package, so they don't dry out and curl up.

1 large medium-ripe mango, cut into small slices

2 4-oz (125 g) wheels of Brie cheese

½ cup (125 mL) toasted pecans, chopped

6 8-inch (20 cm) flour tortillas

vegetable oil or non-stick spray oil for the skillet

1 recipe Cilantro Sour Cream (p. 42)

Serves 8, with 3 wedges per person.

Per wedge: 86 cals, 4.8 g fat, 2.1 g sat. fat, 10 mg cholesterol, 115 mg sodium, 7.3 g carbs, 3.3 g protein

Find 2 similar-shaped tortillas for each quesadilla. Trim the rind from the Brie, removing as little of the cheese as possible, and slice thinly. Divide half of the cheese amongst the 3 "bottom" tortillas. Stay a ½ inch (1 cm) away from the outer edges. Evenly divide the mango between the 3 bases as well, and then the pecans. Top with the remaining cheese and place the top tortillas on each quesadilla.

Heat a large, oiled, non-stick skillet on medium high. Brown one side of the first quesadilla, covered with a lid, for 1 to 2 minutes. The cooked side should be golden and crisp. Slide the quesadilla onto a dinner plate and cover with another plate. Flip over and slide the quesadilla back in the pan, brown the other side for 1 to 2 minutes to finish melting the cheese. Repeat for each quesadilla, oiling the pan in between.

Let the quesadillas rest for 5 minutes to solidify the cheese slightly before cutting. Slice them into 8 wedges and serve warm with sauce on the side.

Makes 24 appetizer pieces.

How to cut a mango
Stand the mango upright with the stem end facing down and slice off the two "cheeks." Cut cheeks into 3 or 4 wedges each. Trim off the two remaining sides and discard the exposed centre core. Peel all the pieces with a sharp knife and slice or dice as required

Roasted Vegetable Bruschetta

You can roast the vegetables ahead of time, and then reheat them in a preheated 350°F (180°C) oven or on the stovetop in a medium skillet.

Preheat the oven to 400°F (200°C).

In a large, shallow baking pan, toss together the vegetables, seasonings, and sugar. Drizzle them with the oil and vinegar; mix well. Bake for 20 minutes, stirring occasionally, until most of the moisture is gone. Roast them until golden, 5 to 8 minutes more, stirring once or twice to ensure even browning. Watch them closely and remove the pan from oven as soon as vegetables are browned.

Preheat the broiler. In a small bowl, mix together the feta, pine nuts, and parsley for the topping.

On a large baking sheet, place the bread slices in a single layer and brush the tops with olive oil. Broil slices for 1 to 2 minutes to toast lightly.

Top each bread slice with the vegetable mixture using about 1 to 1½ tablespoons (15 to 22.5 mL) per slice. Sprinkle 1 teaspoon (5 mL) of the feta-parsley topping on each bruschetta and serve while still warm.

Using Feta cheese

Feta is a Greek cheese made traditionally from sheep's milk but it is now also made domestically from goat or cow's milk. The cheese is stored in a salt brine to help preserve it for a longer period of time. When using feta cheese, rinse it well with cold water and pat it dry with paper towel or you will find the cheese is very salty. Crumble or grate it before using so it incorporates easily into your recipe.

Roasted Vegetables

½ cup (125 mL) onion, diced

½ cup (125 mL) roasted red pepper, diced

⅓ lb (170 g) mushrooms, diced

2 cups (500 mL) eggplant, peeled and diced

¼ tsp (1 mL) salt

¼ tsp (1 mL) pepper

½ tsp (2 mL) sugar

2 Tbsp (30 mL) olive oil

1 Tbsp (15 mL) balsamic vinegar

Topping

2 oz (60 g) feta cheese, at room temperature

¼ cup (60 mL) pine nuts, toasted

1 Tbsp (15 mL) finely minced fresh parsley leaves

Bread

24 ¼-inch (6 mm) slices of French baguette, about 2 × 3-inch (5 × 8 cm) size

2 to 3 Tbsp (30 to 45 mL) olive oil

Makes 24 appetizers.

Per slice (with topping): 66 cals, 3.5 g fat, 0.9 g sat. fat, 2 mg cholesterol, 138 mg sodium, 7 g carbs, 1.6 g protein

Cajun Almond Shrimp

This nutty, spicier version of popcorn shrimp is so addictive!

½ lb (250 g) cooked shrimp, rinsed and dried on a paper towel

1 Tbsp (15 mL) Cajun seasoning

½ cup (125 mL) flour in a medium bowl

1 large egg, beaten, in a medium bowl

¾ cup (185 mL) raw almonds (with skins), ground fine, in a medium bowl

1 cup (250 mL) canola or corn oil for frying

Serves 4.

Per serving: 304 cals, 18.1 g fat, 2 g sat. fat, 164 mg cholesterol, 442 mg sodium, 16.7 g carbs, 18.6 g protein

Put the shrimp in a bowl and sprinkle with Cajun seasoning, tossing them gently to coat thoroughly. Dredge them with the flour, shaking off any excess.

Working with a handful of shrimp at a time, dip the shrimp in the beaten egg. Toss well to coat and then remove using a slotted spoon, letting any excess egg drip back into the bowl. Next, place the shrimp in the nuts and toss them with a spoon to coat well. Set them aside on a plate while coating the rest.

Refrigerate the shrimp, uncovered, for 30 to 60 minutes to help the coating adhere.

In a large, non-stick skillet, heat the oil on medium-high heat until the oil is thoroughly hot but not smoking; it should be rippling. (If uncertain, test the temperature by cooking one shrimp.)

Fry the shrimp briefly, until the coating turns golden brown, about 1 to 2 minutes. Placing onto paper towels to absorb the excess oil and serve immediately.

Mini Crab Cakes with Avocado Sauce

Crab cakes can be prepared and baked ahead of time. Keep refrigerated and bring to room temperature before reheating for 10 minutes in a preheated 350°F (180°F) oven. You can find shelled pistachios in the bulk food section of most grocery stores.

Preheat the oven to 350°F (180°C) and oil a baking sheet with sides.

Place the crabmeat in a medium bowl and discard any shell debris. Add the red pepper, seasonings, nuts, and eggs and mix well. Stir in the fresh breadcrumbs so everything binds together. Form 1¼-inch (3 cm) balls of filling, and press gently to make cakes that are ½-inch (1 cm) thick. (You should get about 2 dozen crab cakes.)

Place the Panko breadcrumbs in a medium bowl. Gently press each crab cake into the breadcrumbs to coat both sides; place on the baking sheet.

Bake crab cakes until firm and pale golden, about 15 minutes. Serve warm with Avocado Sauce on the side.

vegetable oil for baking sheet

1½ cups (375 mL) cooked crabmeat, or 3 6-oz (170 g) cans cocktail crabmeat, drained well

2 Tbsp (30 mL) minced red pepper

1 Tbsp (15 mL) minced fresh parsley leaves

¾ tsp (4 mL) Worcestershire sauce

¾ tsp (4 mL) Chinese chili–garlic sauce

¼ tsp (1 mL) each salt and pepper

⅓ cup (80 mL) toasted pistachios, finely chopped

2 large eggs, beaten

⅓ cup (80 mL) fresh breadcrumbs, or substitute Panko breadcrumbs

1 cup (250 mL) Panko breadcrumbs for coating

1 recipe Avocado Sauce (p. 49)

Makes 24 appetizers.

Per 3 crab cakes (with 6 tsp sauce): 147 cals, 5.4 g fat, 1.1 g sat. fat, 75 mg cholesterol, 350 mg sodium, 14.9 g carbs, 9.8 g protein

Avocado Sauce

In a food processor, purée the avocado with the lime juice until smooth. Add the remaining ingredients and pulse just enough to mix. Place sauce in a container and spread a piece of plastic wrap over the surface to help prevent the sauce from turning brown. Cover with a lid and refrigerate until needed.

1 large avocado, peeled and pitted

1 Tbsp (15 mL) lime juice

¼ tsp each (1 mL) garlic salt, sugar, and pepper

1 Tbsp (15 mL) canned mild green chili peppers, rinsed, dried, and minced

¼ cup (60 mL) trimmed and chopped green onions (about 3)

Makes about 1 cup (250 mL).

Per Tbsp (15 mL): 18 cals, 1.4 g fat, 0.2 g sat. fat, 40 mg sodium, 1 g carbs, 0.2 g protein

Pan-seared Scallops
with Ginger Lime Butter

Serve these scallops as an elegant plated first course, or on an appetizer platter with baguette slices for dipping in the sauce.

Sauce
3 Tbsp (45 mL) lime juice
¼ cup (60 mL) dry white wine
1 tsp (5 mL) minced ginger
¼ tsp (1 mL) minced garlic
¼ tsp (1 mL) pepper
1 Tbsp (15 mL) olive oil
1 tsp (5 mL) sugar
½ cup (125 mL) butter, cold and cut into ¼-inch (6 mm) cubes
⅓ cup (80 mL) roasted, salted pistachios, chopped

Sauce

In a medium skillet, on medium-high heat, bring the lime juice and wine to a boil.

Add the ginger, garlic, and pepper; cook the mixture until almost dry, about 3 to 4 minutes, with only 2 tablespoons (30 mL) remaining in the pan. Add the olive oil, sugar, and mix until smooth. Set aside. (You can make the sauce to this point, cover, and refrigerate until 20 minutes before serving.)

Scallops

Heat a large, non-stick skillet on high heat until very hot; add the oil and butter.

Add the scallops immediately and sear them for 1 to 2 minutes, until very brown, and then turn quickly. Shake the pan to distribute the oil and sear the other side for 1 minute. Remove skillet from heat, cover, and let stand 5 minutes to cook the scallop centres.

Begin warming the sauce on low heat. Gradually whisk in the butter and the nuts. Add the scallops to the sauce and coat them well.

If serving scallops as an appetizer, put them on a plate with a bowl of sauce. Toothpicks or seafood forks can be used for dipping scallops into the sauce. If serving as a first course, divide the spinach or greens between 6 salad plates and top each one with 3 scallops and 2 tablespoons (30 mL) of sauce. Serve immediately!

Scallops

2 Tbsp (30 mL) butter

2 Tbsp (30 mL) olive oil

18 rinsed and dried medium-large scallops (about 1 oz [30 g] each, or 1¼ lb [625 g] total), at room temperature

1½ cups (375 mL) baby spinach leaves or organic greens for serving (optional)

Serves 6, with 3 scallops per person, or 18 appetizers.

Per scallop (with 2 Tbsp [30 mL] sauce): 119 cals, 10 g fat, 4.4 g sat. fat, 26 mg cholesterol, 111 mg sodium, 1.7 g carbs, 5.4 g protein

Skewered Chicken with Peanut Sauce

These skewers are always a big hit at parties! Check your wooden skewers and discard any ones with rough tips or splits in them, and include 4 to 6 extra skewers when you soak them.

4 6-oz (175 g) boneless and skinless chicken breasts (or use 1½ lb [750 g] chicken thighs)

32 8-inch (20 cm) wooden skewers, soaked in warm water for 30 minutes

1 recipe Peanut Sauce (p. 53)

1 Tbsp (15 mL) toasted sesame seeds

Makes 32 skewers.

Per skewer (with 1½ Tbsp [22.5 mL] sauce): 60 cals, 3 g fat, 0.6 g sat. fat, 12 mg cholesterol, 82 mg sodium, 2.1 g carbs, 6.2 g protein

Preheat the oven to 375°F (190°C) and oil a baking sheet.

If Peanut Sauce was made ahead, begin reheating it slowly, stirring frequently because it sticks easily.

Cut the chicken into ¾-inch (2 cm) cubes and spear 2 to 3 onto each skewer.

Bake skewers for 10 minutes, and then check for doneness. (It may take 2 to 3 more minutes in the oven for them to cook through.)

To serve, dip each skewer in the Peanut Sauce and sprinkle with the sesame seeds.

Peanut Sauce

You can use this sauce with skewered chicken, beef, pork, lamb, or vegetables. It also makes an excellent salad dressing when you add 2 tablespoons (30 mL) of water to 1 cup of sauce (250 mL) and whisk until smooth.

In a medium saucepan, combine all the ingredients, except the peanut butter, with ½ cup (125 mL) water. Cook on medium heat for 2 to 3 minutes until the sugar and salt melt.

Turn off the heat and gradually add the peanut butter, alternating with 1 cup (250 mL) water; stir with a whisk until the mixture is smooth and moderately thick. If the sauce is too thick for dipping the skewers, add up to ½ cup (125 mL) more water. While sauce is cooling, stir frequently to prevent a skin from forming on the surface.

⅓ cup (80 mL) packed brown sugar

3 Tbsp (45 mL) lemon juice

1 Tbsp (15 mL) soy sauce

1 tsp (5 mL) minced garlic

1 Tbsp (15 mL) minced ginger

1 tsp (5 mL) salt

½ tsp (2 mL) ground pepper

¼ tsp (1 mL) cayenne pepper

1½ cups (375 mL) smooth peanut butter, preferably Skippy brand

Makes about 3½ cups (875 mL).

Per Tbsp (15 mL): 50 cals, 3.5 g fat, 0.7 g sat. fat, 91 mg sodium, 2.7 g carbs, 1.7 g protein

Honey Nuts and Orange

These nuts can be prepared 2 days ahead of time if stored prior to baking in an airtight container at room temperature. After baking and cooling, a foil- or wax paper–lined tin will help maintain their crunchiness for 5 to 7 days.

1 Tbsp (15 mL) melted butter

¼ cup (60 mL) honey

¼ tsp (1 mL) vanilla

½ tsp (2 mL) cinnamon

½ tsp (2 mL) minced orange zest

1¾ cups (185 mL) whole blanched almonds (or substitute walnuts or pecans)

vegetable oil for baking sheet

salt in a shaker

Makes 2 cups (500 mL).

Per ¼ cup (60 mL): 347 cals, 18.1 g fat, 2.5 g sat. fat, 4 mg cholesterol, 18 mg sodium, 14.5 g carbs, 6.5 g protein

Preheat the oven to 325°F (160°C) and oil a foil-lined baking sheet.

In a medium bowl, mix the melted butter with the honey and flavourings. Add the nuts and stir well to coat them with the glaze. Slide the nut mixture onto the baking sheet and separate the individual nuts as well as you can.

Place the pan on the middle rack of the oven and bake the nuts for 6 to 7 minutes. Remove and stir to ensure even browning and return to the oven for another 6 to 7 minutes. After 12 to 14 minutes, nuts should be deep brown.

Place the baking sheet on a cooling rack and lightly sprinkle the nuts with salt. Cool completely before handling; remove from foil and break apart any connected ones.

Savoury Nut Mix

A perfect snack choice when watching the game, playing darts, or enjoying a movie at home.

Preheat the oven to 300°F (150°C).

In a large bowl, stir the seasonings into the melted butter; add the nuts and mix well. Spread nut mixture on an ungreased baking sheet and bake for 30 minutes, stirring every 10 minutes.

Cool nuts on a rack, then add the raisins, and mix well. Store in an airtight container for up to 2 weeks.

¼ cup (60 mL) melted butter

1 Tbsp (15 mL) soy sauce

1 tsp (5 mL) chili powder

½ tsp (2 mL) garlic salt

¼ tsp (1 mL) cayenne

1 cup (250 mL) raw cashews or pecans

1 cup (250 mL) blanched whole almonds

1 cup (250 mL) raw hazelnuts

1 cup (250 mL) raw peanuts

1 cup (250 mL) raisins

Makes 5 cups.

Per ¼ cup (60 mL): 219 cals, 16.5 g fat, 3.2 g sat. fat, 115 mg sodium, 12.3 g carbs, 5.4 g protein

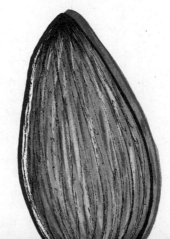

Mexican Nut Mix

Double this one for the holiday party season. It also makes a delicious hostess gift.

Preheat the oven to 375°F (190°C) and prepare an oiled baking sheet.

In a large bowl, mix the nuts and seeds together. Whisk together the other ingredients; pour over the nut mixture and stir well. Spread nut mixture onto the baking sheet and bake for 15 minutes, stirring occasionally.

Cool nuts on the pan on a rack, and then store in an airtight container for up to 2 weeks.

3 cups (750 mL) whole blanched almonds
1½ cups (375 mL) raw sunflower seeds
1½ cups (375 mL) raw shelled pumpkin seeds
2 tsp (10 mL) garlic salt
2 Tbsp (30 mL) chili powder
1 tsp (5 mL) cayenne
2 tsp (10 mL) cumin
1 Tbsp (15 mL) oregano
1 tsp (5 mL) black pepper
2 Tbsp (30 mL) lime juice
¼ cup (60 mL) melted butter

Makes 6 cups (1.5 L).

Per ¼ cup (60 mL): 271 cals, 22.3 g fat, 3.7 g sat. fat, 5 mg cholesterol, 31 mg sodium, 7.5 g carbs, 9.9 g protein

salads

Marinated Fennel with Almonds

Gourmet coleslaw!

2 medium lemons

3 large Gala or Fuji apples

2 medium fennel bulbs, greens removed and trimmed of any brown spots

2 Tbsp (30 mL) sugar

2 minced shallots (about ¼ cup [60 mL])

¼ tsp (1 mL) salt

¼ tsp (1 mL) pepper

¼ cup (60 mL) almond oil

½ cup (125 mL) toasted sliced almonds

1 Tbsp (15 mL) minced fresh parsley

Serves 6.

Per serving: 211 cals, 13.5 g fat, 1.1 g sat. fat, 122 mg sodium, 20.1 g carbs, 2.2 g protein

Zest both the lemons into a deep bowl. Cut the lemons in half, juice them, and strain the liquid into the bowl to remove any seeds.

Quarter and core the apples before slicing them thin and adding them to the lemon juice mixture. Quarter the fennel bulbs vertically and remove the core before cutting the pieces horizontally into thin slices. Add the fennel slices, sugar, shallots, salt, and pepper to the lemon mixture; stir well.

Let the salad marinate for 10 to 15 minutes to dissolve the sugar. Add the almond oil and mix well. Cover and refrigerate for several hours, stirring occasionally.

Remove the salad from the fridge 30 minutes before serving and stir well. Just prior to serving, top the salad with the toasted almonds and minced parsley.

Cooking Tip:

If you do not have almond oil, substitute canola or corn oil.

Asparagus and Avocado Salad with Bacon Cashew Vinaigrette

My favourite salad in this book!

Chop the bacon into ½-inch (1 cm) pieces and refrigerate until needed.

Fill a large pot with water and bring it to a boil. Add the asparagus and blanch for 1 minute, until it turns bright green. Drain the asparagus in a colander and rinse with cold water to stop the cooking. Dry off the spears and divide them among 4 plates, creating a semicircle or fan shape.

Halve avocadoes, and then slice each half lengthwise into 4 wedges. Dip each wedge in lemon juice, or sprinkle with Fruit-Fresh®, to prevent browning and place 4 wedges between the 5 asparagus spears on each plate.

Warm the bacon and cashews briefly in a medium skillet on medium heat for 2 to 3 minutes. Sprinkle each plate with a quarter of the bacon/nut mix and drizzle each salad with Sherry Vinaigrette. Serve immediately.

Cutting an avocado

Choose avocadoes that are medium ripe. They should be slightly soft when pressed but still somewhat firm. They won't slice well if they are ripe or mushy (use those ones for Avocado Sauce [p. 49]).

To prep each avocado, start with the stem end pointing up. Slice through the skin from top to bottom, rotating the avocado away from you as you slice lengthwise around the pit. Pick up the avocado and twist your hands in opposite directions to separate it into two halves. Carefully poke the tip of a knife into the pit; remove and discard. Scoop out the inner pulp from the two sides with a spoon, aiming to keep each half in one piece. Slice or dice as required for the recipe.

4 thick-cut slices or 8 thin slices of bacon, cooked until crisp

20 pencil-sized spears of asparagus, trimmed to 5 inches (12 cm) long

2 medium or large avocadoes, ripe but still tender firm

lemon juice or Fruit-Fresh® Produce Protector for coating avocado wedges

1 recipe Sherry Vinaigrette (p. 60)

¼ cup (60 mL) toasted cashews, chopped

Serves 4.

Per serving (with 2 Tbsp [30 mL] dressing): 584 cals, 51.5 g fat, 10.3 g sat. fat, 24 mg cholesterol, 699 mg sodium, 15.7 g carbs, 14 g protein

Sherry Vinaigrette

This dressing is fantastic when made with 30-year-old Spanish sherry vinegar—they'll wipe the plate clean. However, you can substitute a younger sherry vinegar, or white balsamic vinegar, and it's still very good. This vinaigrette also makes a great bread dipper! It can be made up to 2 days ahead.

Whisk all the ingredients together, except the oil, until the salt and sugar dissolve. Whisk in the oil by hand only until just blended; if you blend it using a machine it will be too thick.

Cover and refrigerate for 1 to 2 hours so the flavours blend. Bring dressing to room temperature to serve.

2 Tbsp (30 mL) sherry vinegar
(or substitute white balsamic vinegar)
1 small shallot, minced (about 2 Tbsp [30 mL])
1 Tbsp (15 mL) Dijon mustard
¼ tsp (1 mL) salt
¼ tsp (1 mL) pepper
2 tsp (10 mL) sugar
⅓ cup (80 mL) olive oil

Makes ½ cup (125 mL).

Per Tbsp (15 mL): 89 cals, 9.2 g fat, 1.2 g sat. fat,
117 mg sodium, 1.4 g carbs, 0.2 g protein

Couscous Salad with Fresh Mango and Toasted Pistachios

Unique, colourful, and flavourful. Great as a side dish with grilled chicken or as a buffet salad for a party!

Fill a large bowl with the water and soak the couscous, covered. In a separate large bowl, place the chopped vegetables, fruit, and pistachios.

After 5 minutes, fluff the couscous with a fork before adding it to the bowl with the other ingredients. Add the vinaigrette and cilantro; mix well.

1½ cups (375 mL) boiling water

1½ cups (375 mL) plain couscous

½ bunch green onions (about 3), trimmed and sliced ¼-inch (6 mm) thick on an angle

½ a head of radicchio, coarsely chopped

2 large mangoes, peeled and cut into ½-inch (1 cm) cubes

½ cup (125 mL) golden raisins

½ cup (125 mL) toasted pistachios

1 recipe Mango Vinaigrette (p. 61)

2 Tbsp (30 mL) minced fresh cilantro leaves

Serves 6.

Per serving: 487 cals, 24.3 g fat, 2 g sat. fat, 207 mg sodium, 59 g carbs, 8.1 g protein

Mango Vinaigrette

A light, refreshing choice for any green salad with fruit and, of course, toasted nuts! If you can't find mango vinegar, substitute 2 tablespoons (30 mL) white balsamic vinegar and 2 tablespoons (30 mL) mango purée.

Mix the vinegar with the sugar and seasonings for 1 to 2 minutes to dissolve the sugar and the salt. Gradually whisk in the oil.

¼ cup (60 mL) mango vinegar, preferably Mediterranean Jewel brand

1 Tbsp (15 mL) sugar

½ tsp (2 mL) salt

½ tsp (2 mL) pepper

½ cup (125 mL) canola oil

Makes ¾ cup (185 mL).

Per Tbsp (15 mL): 90 cals, 9.1 g fat, 0.6 g sat. fat, 98 mg sodium, 1.9 g carbs

Cranberry and Hazelnut Salad with Raspberry Vinaigrette

A healthy, seasonal choice at Christmas or Easter before your roast turkey dinner. Doubles and triples easily.

3 Tbsp (45 mL) raspberry vinegar
1 Tbsp (15 mL) Dijon mustard
2 Tbsp (30 mL) honey
¼ tsp (1 mL) pepper
½ tsp (2 mL) salt
½ cup (125 mL) olive oil
2 tsp (10 mL) minced fresh tarragon
8 cups (2 L) mixed salad greens
½ cup (125 mL) toasted blanched hazelnuts, chopped
½ cup (125 mL) dried cranberries

Serves 4.

Per serving: 411 cals, 33.8 g fat, 4 g sat. fat, 391 mg sodium, 24 g carbs, 3 g protein

In a large bowl, whisk the vinegar, mustard, honey, and seasonings together. Add the oil gradually, whisking until incorporated, then stir in the tarragon.

Add the greens to the dressing and toss to coat well, then divide between the 4 plates. Top with hazelnuts and cranberries prior to serving.

Orange and Pecan Salad
with Champagne Vinaigrette

This salad is fresh, cool, and crisp! It works well with summer or winter meals because the ingredients are always available.

Oranges

Slice the top and bottom ½ inch (1 cm) off the oranges. Slice off the peel, cutting from top to bottom, until you see the flesh. Continue cutting top to bottom, around the orange, until only flesh remains without any white pith.

Over a medium bowl, with a sharp paring knife, wedge out the orange segents, avoiding the dividing membranes and saving 2 tablespoons (30 mL) juice for the dressing. With a sieve, drain any juice off the oranges.

Vinaigrette

In a medium bowl, mix together all of the dressing ingredients, except the oil. Stir until the salt and sugar dissolve. Drizzle in the oil while whisking the mixture (this step can be done by hand or in a food processor).

Salad

Divide the greens evenly between 6 plates and top each one with a sixth of the drained oranges, pecans, and onion slices. Just prior to serving, drizzle each salad with 2½ tablespoons (37.5 mL) of dressing.

Oranges

3 large navel oranges

Vinaigrette

2 Tbsp (30 mL) champagne vinegar
(or substitute white wine vinegar)

2 Tbsp (30 mL) orange juice, reserved
from the prepared oranges

2 tsp (10 mL) sugar

½ tsp (2 mL) salt

½ tsp (2 mL) pepper

½ cup (125 mL) canola oil

Salad

9 cups (2.25 L) Romaine lettuce, spinach, or mixed greens, small leaves or torn into bite-sized pieces

½ cup (125 mL) toasted pecan halves

½ a small red onion, quartered,
core removed, and thinly sliced

Serves 6.

Per serving (including dressing): 281 cals, 25.1 g fat,
1.8 g sat. fat, 203 mg sodium, 11 g carbs, 2.8 g protein

New Potato Salad with Red Onion and Hazelnuts

A delicious, hearty addition to any barbecue or buffet.

3 lb (1.5 kg) baby potatoes or new potatoes

2 Tbsp (30 mL) white wine vinegar or white balsamic vinegar

1 Tbsp plus 1 tsp (20 mL) sugar

1 Tbsp (15 mL) grainy Dijon mustard

½ tsp (2 mL) salt

½ tsp (2 mL) pepper

⅓ cup (80 mL) canola oil

⅓ cup (80 mL) olive oil

2 Tbsp (30 mL) fresh parsley, minced

2 Tbsp (30 mL) dry white wine

1 medium red onion, peeled and trimmed

1 cup (250 mL) toasted blanched hazelnuts, coarsely chopped

Serves 8.

Per serving: 428 cals, 27.5 g fat, 2.5 g sat. fat, 202 mg sodium, 39 g carbs, 6 g protein

Cut the baby potatoes in half, or larger potatoes into quarters, for even-sized chunks. Prepare a steamer or bring a large pot of salted water to a rolling boil. Add the potatoes and cook until tender. They will take 10 to 20 minutes depending on their size.

While the potatoes are cooking, whisk together the vinegar and sugar in a deep, medium bowl. Add the mustard and seasoning; mix well to dissolve the sugar. Gradually whisk in the oils and the parsley; set aside.

Cut the onion into quarters, and then slice it very thin, until almost see-through, using a food processor, a mandolin, or by hand. Add the onions to the dressing to marinate them.

Once the potatoes are cooked, sprinkle them with the white wine while still warm. Cool them to room temperature, then add them to the onion mixture and stir gently to coat.

Cover and refrigerate until 30 minutes before serving. Add ¾ cup (185 mL) hazelnuts just before serving and stir gently. Garnish salad with the remaining ¼ cup (60 mL) of nuts.

Strawberry and Almond Salad with Balsamic Vinaigrette

Strawberries, sweet crunchy almonds, and Balsamic dressing—could it get any better?

In a medium bowl, whisk the sugar and seasonings into the vinegar until dissolved. Use the whisk to gradually stir in the oils but do not beat or the dressing will become very thick. Cover and refrigerate until ready to serve.

Top the spinach with sliced strawberries, then add the dressing and toss well. Divide the mixture between 8 plates.

Sprinkle each portion with a half-teaspoon (2 mL) of poppy seeds and 2 tablespoons (30 mL) Glazed Balsamic Almonds. Serve immediately.

3 Tbsp (45 mL) balsamic vinegar

1 tsp (5 mL) sugar

½ tsp (2 mL) salt

½ tsp (2 mL) pepper

½ cup (125 mL) canola oil

¼ cup (60 mL) almond oil (or substitute canola oil)

2 heads spinach or 12 cups (3 L) spinach leaves, small leaves or torn into bite-sized pieces

2 lb (1 kg) fresh strawberries, hulled and sliced

1 cup (250 mL) Glazed Balsamic Almonds (p. 66)

1 Tbsp plus 1 tsp (20 mL) poppy seeds

Serves 8.

Per serving: 414 cals, 35.6 g fat, 2.9 g sat. fat, 256 mg sodium, 15.8 g carbs, 6.9 g protein

Glazed Balsamic Almonds

These almonds are one of the tastiest candied nuts I have ever had, and they are very easy to make! You will love the sweet and salty combination. These nuts can be made up to 2 days ahead of time if stored in an airtight container at room temperature. A foil- or wax paper–lined tin will keep them for 5 to 7 days. (But, trust me, they won't be around for that long!)

½ cup (125 mL) sugar
2 Tbsp (30 mL) balsamic vinegar
¼ tsp (1 mL) pepper
1¾ cups (435 mL) whole blanched almonds
vegetable oil
salt in a shaker

Makes 2¼ cups (560 mL).

Per ¼ cup (60 mL): 178 cals, 14.8 g fat, 1.4 g sat. fat, 36 mg sodium, 5.4 g carbs, 5.8 g protein

Preheat the oven to 325°F (160°C) and oil a foil-lined baking sheet.

In a large, non-stick skillet, combine the sugar, vinegar, and pepper. Cook on medium heat until the sugar dissolves; add the nuts and mix well. Slide the nut mixture onto the baking sheet and separate the nuts as well as you can.

Place in the oven on the middle rack and bake the nuts for 6 to 7 minutes. Remove and stir to ensure even browning; bake another 6 to 7 minutes until nuts turn deep brown, 12 to 14 minutes total.

Place the baking sheet onto a cooling rack and sprinkle the nuts lightly with salt. Cool completely before handling, then remove the nuts from the foil and break apart any connected ones.

Pear and Candied Walnut Salad with Dijon Wine Vinaigrette

A great flavour combo and a fantastic accompaniment to Pecan Coated Pork Chops (p. 82).

In a medium bowl, whisk together the vinegar, mustard, sugar, and seasoning. Gradually whisk in the oil and mix until the sugar dissolves.

Peel, core, and slice the pears ½-inch (1 cm) thick. Add them to the dressing and stir gently to coat them well.

Divide the greens between 6 plates. Top each one with a sixth of the pear slices. Drizzle with remaining dressing and sprinkle with 2 tablespoons (30 mL) of candied nuts. Serve immediately.

2 Tbsp (30 mL) red wine vinegar

1 Tbsp (15 mL) Dijon mustard

1 Tbsp plus 1 tsp (20 mL) sugar

½ tsp (2 mL) salt

¼ tsp (1 mL) pepper

⅔ cup (160 mL) canola oil

3 large Bartlett pears, medium ripe

1 large head of romaine or green leaf lettuce, chopped or torn into bite-sized pieces

1 cup (250 mL) Candied Walnuts (p. 68)

Serves 6.

Per serving: 454 cals, 38.4 g fat, 2.9 g sat. fat, 264 mg sodium, 22.2 g carbs, 4.9 g protein

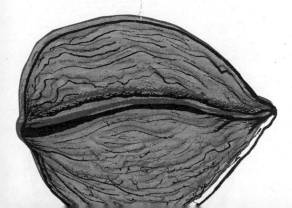

Candied Walnuts

This recipe got me excited about using walnuts because they turn out so delicate and crisp! These nuts are easy to make and you can make them ahead of time but make sure you hide them well. They should last up to 2 weeks if stored properly but this has never been tested because they are always completely gone within a few days.

Have the sugar ready in a medium bowl to use after the nuts are blanched. In a medium saucepan, bring a pot of water to a full boil. Add the walnuts and boil for 1 minute, then drain and rinse well with hot water. Toss the warm walnuts in the sugar to coat well and dissolve the sugar a bit.

Heat 1 inch (2.5 cm) of oil in a medium-large skillet on medium-high heat until hot; add the nuts. Cook them, stirring frequently, until evenly golden in colour, about 5 minutes. Drain fried nuts on paper towels. If they are for snacking, sprinkle lightly with salt; if they are intended for a salad containing fresh fruit, omit the salt. Nuts will firm up as they cool and develop a light crunch. Store them in a covered container (a tin works well).

¼ cup (60 mL) sugar
2 cups (500 mL) walnut halves
½ cup (125 mL) vegetable oil
salt (optional)

Makes 2 cups (500 mL).

Per ¼ cup (60 mL) serving: 246 cals, 20.3 g fat, 1.8 g sat. fat, 3 mg sodium, 11.7 g carbs, 4.3 g protein

Cooking Tip:
This recipe doubles or triples easily if you fry the nuts in batches.

Dijon Chicken Salad
with Cucumber and Cashews

Fresh, crunchy, and creamy!

In a large bowl, combine the chicken, cucumber, green onions, and celery.

In a separate, smaller bowl, whisk together the lemon juice, mustard, and honey. Add the seasonings and then whisk in the mayonnaise and the parsley.

Stir the dressing into the chicken mixture and combine to coat everything well. Cover and refrigerate to blend the flavours. Just before serving, add the cashews and stir well.

2 cups (500 mL) cooked chicken, cubed

½ cup (125 mL) English cucumber, cubed and dried off with a paper towel

¼ cup (60 mL) green onions (about 3), sliced ¼-inch (6 mm) thick on an angle

½ cup (125 mL) diced celery (about 1 medium-small stalk)

1 Tbsp (15 mL) lemon juice

2 Tbsp (30 mL) Dijon mustard

2 Tbsp (30 mL) honey

½ tsp (2 mL) salt

¼ tsp (1 mL) pepper

¼ tsp (1 mL) cayenne

1 cup (250 mL) mayonnaise

1 Tbsp (15 mL) fresh parsley, minced

½ cup (125 mL) toasted cashews, chopped

Serves 4 as a salad entree over greens, or 6 if used as the filling for Dijon Chicken Salad Croissants (p. 33).

Per entree-sized serving: 620 cals, 50.8 g fat, 6.2 g sat. fat, 74 mg cholesterol, 908 mg sodium, 16 .5 g carbs, 24.2 g protein

Thai Chicken and Cashew Noodle Salad

Healthy, low-fat, and full of flavour!

4 7-oz (200 g) bundles of instant Asian egg noodles

1 bunch green onions (about 6), sliced thin on an angle

2 medium carrots, peeled, trimmed, and coarsely grated or cut into matchstick-sized pieces

1 cup (250 mL) asparagus or snow peas, trimmed and cut ¼-inch (6 mm) thick on an angle

2 Tbsp (30 mL) toasted sesame seeds

1 recipe Low-Fat Thai Dressing (p. 70)

2 8-oz (250 g) boneless and skinless cooked chicken breasts

2 medium tomatoes, cut into ½-inch (1 cm) cubes

⅓ cup (80 mL) toasted cashews, chopped

2 Tbsp (30 mL) minced fresh cilantro leaves

Serves 4 as a main dish.

Per serving: 452 cals, 9.7 g fat, 1.6 g sat. fat, 32 mg cholesterol, 768 mg sodium, 70.1 g carbs, 21 g protein

Bring a large pot of water to a boil; add the noodles and cook according to package directions. This step usually takes 2 to 5 minutes depending on the brand. Drain the noodles, rinse them with cold water, and drain again.

In a large bowl, combine the noodles with the onions, carrots, asparagus or snow peas, and sesame seeds. Mix in a third of the dressing, and then heap the mixture onto a serving dish.

Slice the chicken breasts into 2- to 3-inch (5 to 8 cm) long strips, approximately 1 inch (2.5 cm) wide and ¼ inch (6 mm) thick. Fan the chicken slices out on top of the noodles. Top the chicken with a row of fresh tomato cubes, nuts, and cilantro. Drizzle with the remaining dressing just prior to serving.

Low-Fat Thai Dressing

You can also brush this dressing on grilled vegetables or kebabs to add flavour.

¼ cup (60 mL) rice vinegar (or white vinegar)

2 Tbsp (30 mL) each lemon juice and oyster juice

2 Tbsp (30 mL) honey

½ tsp (2 mL) each sesame oil and minced garlic

1 tsp (5 mL) minced ginger

¼ tsp (1 mL) salt

½ tsp (2 mL) pepper

Makes ⅔ cup (160 mL).

Per Tbsp (15 mL): 21 cals, 0.2 g fat, 74 mg sodium, 4.6 g carbs, 0.1 g protein

Whisk all the ingredients together in a medium bowl and refrigerate, covered, for 1 to 2 hours to blend the flavours.

Marinated Cheese and Walnut Salad

My version of the traditional Italian cheese salad.

Wash, trim, quarter, and core the fennel bulbs, and then slice thinly. Three bulbs should yield 8 to 9 cups (2 to 2.25 L) of slices. Cut the cheese into 2-inch (5 cm) julienne strips, about ¼-inch (6 mm) wide. Combine the cheese, fennel, and parsley in a large shallow dish.

In a medium bowl, combine the lemon juice, sugar, salt, and pepper. Whisk well to dissolve the sugar and salt. Whisk in the olive oil, and then pour it over the dish with the fennel and cheese slices. Stir gently to coat well.

Cover and marinate for 2 to 3 hours. Bring to room temperature before serving and top with the walnuts.

3 large fennel bulbs

1 lb (500 g) Edam cheese, preferably from New Zealand

2 Tbsp (30 mL) minced fresh parsley

¼ cup (60 mL) fresh lemon juice

2 Tbsp (30 mL) sugar

¼ tsp (1 mL) salt

¼ tsp (1 mL) pepper

¼ cup (60 mL) olive oil

¾ cup (185 mL) toasted walnut halves

Serves 8.

Per serving: 376 cals, 30.9 g fat, 10 g sat. fat, 38 mg cholesterol, 553 mg sodium, 9.2 g carbs, 15.3 g protein

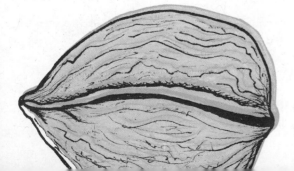

Main Dishes

Baked Macaroni and Cheese with Nut Crust

A super-tasty version of mac and cheese to enjoy!

Macaroni

1 lb (500 g) dried macaroni
1 Tbsp (15 mL) salt

Cheese Sauce

¼ cup (60 mL) butter
¼ cup (60 mL) flour
¼ cup (60 mL) white wine
1 cup (250 mL) whipping cream
1 tsp (5 mL) Dijon mustard
½ tsp (2 mL) garlic salt
½ tsp (2 mL) pepper
¼ tsp (1 mL) ground nutmeg
1 tsp (5 mL) Tabasco sauce (or ½ tsp [2 mL] Chinese chili–garlic sauce)
3 cups (750 mL) grated sharp cheddar cheese

Macaroni

Heat a large pot of water to boiling; add the salt. Add the macaroni and stir well; boil until al dente (slightly chewy), stirring occasionally. (Check the pasta packaging for the recommended cooking time.)

Cheese Sauce

Melt the butter in a medium-large saucepan on medium heat. Add the flour; cook for 1 to 2 minutes, whisking the mixture to blend it. Add the wine and whisk until smooth. Pour in the cream and cook until the sauce thickens.

Add 2 cups (500 mL) of water gradually, whisking frequently to prevent lumping. Cook for 10 to 15 minutes until the sauce thickens, continuing to whisk frequently.

Add the seasoning, mustard, and Tabasco followed by 2 cups (500 mL) of cheddar cheese. Mix well and cook until the cheese is melted, about 2 to 3 minutes.

Topping

In a medium bowl, mix the Panko breadcrumbs with the nuts, olive oil, and melted butter. Set aside.

Assembly

Preheat the oven to 375°F (190°C) and oil a 3-quart (3 L) baking dish.

Drain the pasta and rinse it with hot water. Shake off the excess water before mixing the pasta into the sauce and pouring it into the baking dish. Evenly distribute the remaining cup of grated cheddar over the macaroni and sprinkle the cheese layer with the breadcrumb mixture, plus paprika and/or dried parsley (if desired) for colour.

Bake the pasta for 20 to 30 minutes, to crisp the topping and brown the edges.

Topping

¾ cup (185 mL) Panko breadcrumbs

¾ cup (185 mL) raw ground nuts
(ground almonds or pecans work well)

1 Tbsp (15 mL) olive oil

1 Tbsp (15 mL) melted butter

paprika and dried parsley for garnishing

Serves 6.

Per serving: 927 cals, 56.1 g fat, 29.8 g sat. fat, 147 mg cholesterol, 681 g sodium, 74.1 g carbs, 31.6 g protein

Chicken Scaloppine
with Roasted Tomato Sauce

This dish pairs well with a side of pasta and green beans, broccoli, or asparagus for a vegetable. Serve with Angel Hair Pasta with Basil Pesto (p. 94) for a colourful Italian-style dinner.

Cut each chicken breast horizontally into four slices, about ⅓- to ½-inch (8 mm to 1 cm) thick. With a smooth mallet, pound each slice, between sheets of wax paper, to ¼-inch (6 mm) thickness. Sprinkle the sides of each slice with salt and pepper.

Mix the breadcrumbs and the almonds together in a medium bowl and have the beaten egg ready in another medium bowl. Shake off the excess flour from the chicken before dipping each slice in the egg, letting any excess run off. Coat each egg-dipped slice with enough crumb mixture to cover completely. Place the breaded chicken slices on a plate and refrigerate for 30 to 60 minutes, uncovered, so the coating can set and stay adhered when fried.

Preheat the oven to 250°F (120°C), for keeping the chicken warm while frying batches.

In a large and deep, non-stick skillet, heat ½-inch (1 cm) of oil on medium-high heat until it starts rippling. Do not crowd the chicken: cook in 2 batches. Fry the breasts until golden brown and cooked through, turning once. This will only take about 2 to 3 minutes per side. Drain them on paper towels and keep warm in the oven.

Drizzle with warm Roasted Tomato Sauce and sprinkle with grated Parmesan cheese if desired.

2 8-oz (250 g) boneless and skinless chicken breasts

salt and pepper in shakers

⅓ cup (80 mL) flour

½ cup (125 mL) Panko breadcrumbs

½ cup (125 mL) ground almonds

1 large egg, beaten

1 cup (250 mL) canola oil or corn oil for frying

1 recipe Roasted Tomato Sauce (p. 77) (or substitute purchased tomato-basil sauce)

grated Parmesan cheese for garnishing (optional)

Serves 4, with 2 pieces of chicken per person.

Per serving (with ¼ cup [60 mL] sauce): 559 cals, 29.5 g fat, 4.4 g sat. fat, 155 mg cholesterol, 428 mg sodium, 26.2 g carbs, 46.6 g protein

Roasted Tomato Sauce

Make plenty of sauce in the fall when tomatoes are abundant and inexpensive. I can it in jars so it is always available—it tastes just like fresh sauce when opened.

Preheat the oven to 375°F (190°C) and oil a large 2-inch-deep (5 cm) baking dish.

Cut the tomatoes in half horizontally. Place them skin side down in the pan and drizzle with olive oil. Really coat them and let the oil get under and around the tomato halves. Sprinkle tomatoes liberally with the garlic salt, pepper, and oregano.

Bake for 30 to 40 minutes; tomatoes are ready when the skins start pulling away from the flesh. Cool for at least 15 minutes before removing the skins.

Discard the skins and scrape the tomatoes, juice, and oil into the bowl of a food processor. Pulse several times to coarsely chop the tomatoes. The sauce formed should be chunky but rich and almost creamy from the oil. Add the sugar and the basil. Taste the sauce and add more salt if needed.

12 large Roma tomatoes
¼ cup (60 mL) olive oil
garlic salt and pepper in shakers
1 tsp (5 mL) dried oregano flakes, crushed in your palm or crumbled with your fingers
1 tsp (5 mL) sugar
2 Tbsp (30 mL) fresh basil, minced

Makes 3 cups (750 mL).

Per ¼ cup (60 mL) serving: 104 cals, 9.3 g fat, 1.2 g sat. fat, 57 mg sodium, 4.2 g carbs, 0.7 g protein

Cooking Tip:

This recipe can be easily doubled or tripled, and also freezes well.

Cashew Glazed Salmon

Cheddar Potatoes with Almond Crust (p. 98) is an excellent accompaniment to this dish.

¼ cup (60 mL) brown sugar

1 Tbsp (15 mL) lemon juice

¼ tsp (1 mL) Tabasco sauce

1 tsp (5 mL) soy sauce

1½ lb (750 g) full side fillet of salmon, boneless, skin on

2 Tbsp (30 mL) toasted sesame seeds

½ cup (125 mL) toasted cashews, chopped

Serves 4.

Per 6-oz (175 g) fish serving: 375 cals, 16 g fat, 2.8 g sat. fat, 89 mg cholesterol, 211 mg sodium, 20.5 g carbs, 37.3 g protein

Preheat the oven to 375°F (190°C) and oil a baking dish that will fit the fish.

Place the salmon in the baking dish, skin side down. Cut slashes in the fish 2 inches (5 cm) apart and ½ inch (1 cm) deep but do not cut completely through the fillet.

In a small bowl, mix the sugar with the lemon juice, Tabasco, and soy sauce; pour over the salmon.

Bake the salmon, uncovered, for 10 to 20 minutes. (Allow 10 minutes per inch of thickness so salmon is cooked thoroughly but still be moist.) Just before serving, sprinkle with sesame seeds and toasted cashews.

Cashew Peppered Prawns

Present these prawns on a bed of rice or serve with noodles and Asian greens for a fast and easy dinner.

In a medium-large, non-stick skillet on medium heat, mix together the brown sugar, garlic, oyster sauce, and pepper. Cook for 1 to 2 minutes until the sugar is dissolved.

Add the prawns and cook for 2 to 3 minutes more, stirring constantly, until heated through. Just before serving, sprinkle with the cilantro and the cashews.

2 Tbsp (30 mL) packed brown sugar

1 tsp (5 mL) minced garlic

⅓ cup (80 mL) oyster sauce

2 tsp (10 mL) coarse cracked pepper

1 lb (500 g) cooked prawns (about 30 to 40), peeled and de-veined

1 Tbsp (15 mL) minced fresh cilantro leaves

¼ cup (60 mL) toasted cashews, chopped

Serves 6.

Per serving (about 6 prawns): 134 cals, 3.9 g fat, 0.7 g sat. fat, 113 mg cholesterol, 212 mg sodium, 8.2 g carbs, 16.4 g protein

Glazed Bison Kebabs
with Almond Shallot Wine Sauce

Try these kebabs with Barley Pilaf with Chestnuts (p. 102) for a robust fall dinner. You can substitute beef for the bison in this recipe if desired.

Kebabs
Trim any fat from the steaks. Pepper both sides and cut into 2-inch (5 cm) cubes; place in a baking dish.

Glazing and Assembly
In a small bowl, mix the vinegar and the maple syrup. Pour it over the steak pieces and mix well. Skewer the steak, placing 3 to 4 pieces on each skewer. Marinate the kebabs in the reserved glaze until ready to cook. Preparing the skewers can be done earlier in the day. Just cover them and refrigerate until 30 minutes before grilling.

Sauce
In a medium skillet, cook the shallots in the beef stock on medium heat until transparent, about 3 to 5 minutes, stirring occasionally. Add the garlic; cook 1 to 2 minutes more. Pour in the Almond Wine Sauce and stir to combine. Reduce heat to low. Slowly heat the sauce for about 10 minutes, stirring frequently so it doesn't stick.

Cooking
Oil the barbecue grill and preheat to medium-high. If broiling, oil a baking sheet for the kebabs instead. Grill or broil the kebabs to your liking; medium-rare takes 2 to 3 minutes per side if they are within 3 inches (8 cm) of the heat source. (Remember that the kebabs will continue to cook after removed from heat.) While they are cooking, brush kebabs with remaining glaze. Serve with the warm sauce on the side for dipping.

Kebabs

4 7-oz (200 g) Bison striploin or sirloin steaks

freshly ground pepper in a mill or shaker

Glaze

¼ cup (60 mL) Balsamic vinegar

¼ cup (60 mL) maple syrup

12 8-inch (20 cm) bamboo skewers, presoaked in water for 30 minutes

Sauce

½ cup (125 mL) beef stock

2 shallots, peeled and minced (about ¼ cup [60 mL])

½ tsp (2 mL) minced garlic

1 recipe Almond Wine Sauce (p. 81)

vegetable oil for barbecue grill or baking sheet

Serves 4, with 3 skewers each.

Per serving with 3 Tbsp (45 mL) sauce: 494 cals, 28.6 g fat, 14.5 g sat. fat, 168 mg cholesterol, 376 mg sodium, 20.6 g carbs, 38.3 g protein

Almond Wine Sauce

This is an extremely rich, smooth, sexy sauce!

Melt the butter in a medium saucepan on medium heat; add the flour. Cook, stirring with a whisk, for 1 to 2 minutes before whisking in the wine and mustard. Add the seasoning and about ¾ cup (185 mL) of the whipping cream to the pan; whisk well.

Cook the sauce until it thickens, about 5 minutes, whisking frequently to prevent lumping. Occasionally scrape the bottom edges of the pan with a spatula.

In a small bowl, whisk the remaining cream with the almond butter until smooth. Strain it into the sauce, stirring constantly until incorporated.

¼ cup (60 mL) butter

¼ cup (60 mL) flour

¼ cup (60 mL) dry white wine

½ tsp (2 mL) Dijon mustard

¼ tsp (1 mL) salt

¼ tsp (1 mL) pepper

1 cup (250 mL) whipping cream, at room temperature

2 tsp (10 mL) almond butter

Makes 1½ cups (375 mL).

Per Tbsp (15 mL): 77 cals, 7.4 g fat, 4.1 g sat. fat, 22 mg cholesterol, 59 mg sodium, 1.8 g carbs, 0.6 g protein

Pecan Coated Pork Chops with Tabasco Applesauce

The crispy breading helps to keep the chops moist and it is also super-tasty. This dish pairs well with Squash and Pecan Risotto (p. 105).

¼ cup (60 mL) ground pecans

1 cup (250 mL) Panko breadcrumbs

¼ cup (60 mL) flour

4 1-inch (2.5 cm) thick double-loin pork chops

salt and pepper in shakers or grinders

1 large egg

1 cup (250 mL) canola oil for frying

1 cup (250 mL) unsweetened applesauce

½ tsp (2 mL) Tabasco sauce

Serves 4.

Per chop with ¼ cup (60 mL) applesauce: 572 cals, 24.3 g fat, 5.8 g sat. fat, 196 mg cholesterol, 370 mg sodium, 34.1 g carbs, 54.2 g protein

Cooking Tip:

You can freeze uncooked breaded pork chops: layer with waxed paper and stack in an airtight container or freezer bag. They will keep up to 3 months in the freezer if wrapped well.

Preheat the oven to 325°F (160°C) and oil a baking sheet.

In a medium bowl, mix the pecans and the breadcrumbs. Place the flour in another medium bowl. In a third medium bowl, beat the egg until frothy. Dry off the chops with paper towel, and salt and pepper both sides of each chop.

Dredge the chops in flour and shake off any excess. One at a time, dip each chop in the egg, coating it well and letting any excess drain back into the bowl, and then coat thoroughly with the crumb mixture. Set aside on a plate. Repeat until all four chops are breaded; refrigerate, uncovered, for at least 30 minutes or up to several hours. Bring them to room temperature before frying.

Lightly oil a baking dish that can fit all 4 chops in a single layer. In a large, non-stick skillet on medium-high heat, heat the oil. Fry each of the chops in the hot oil and cook until golden brown, about 5 minutes per side. Don't overcrowd them: cook in 2 batches if necessary.

Place fried chops on the oiled sheet and bake until cooked through, about 25 to 30 minutes. While they are baking, mix the applesauce with the Tabasco sauce in a small bowl.

Serve chops with sauce on the side.

Meatballs in Curried Peanut Sauce

These meatballs make a delicious mid-week dinner when served with rice and snap or snow peas.

Mix the ground meat with the onions, salt, and pepper. Use your hands to make small meatballs, about 1 inch in diameter. Dredge them in the flour, shaking off any excess.

In a large, non-stick skillet, heat 2 tablespoons (30 mL) oil on medium-high. Fry the meatballs until golden, about 3 to 4 minutes per side. Cook them in several batches if necessary. Remove them from the skillet and set aside on a plate.

Reduce heat to medium and add 1 tablespoon (15 mL) oil to the skillet. Fry the curry paste with the garlic until aromatic (about 1 to 2 minutes), stirring frequently to prevent sticking.

In a small bowl, whisk the coconut powder with ½ cup (125 mL) of water to make a cream or spoon off ½ cup (125 mL) of thick coconut cream from the top of the canned coconut milk, reserving the milk for thinning your sauce.

Add the coconut cream, oyster sauce, and sugar to the skillet; whisk well. Add the peanut butter and whisk until smooth; the sauce should be like thick gravy. If the sauce is too thick, add tablespoonfuls of water or coconut milk until you achieve the desired consistency.

Return the meatballs to the skillet and stir to coat them with the sauce. Sprinkle with fresh cilantro or basil just before serving.

1 lb (500 g) lean ground veal or ground pork

¼ cup (60 mL) minced onion

1½ tsp (7.5 mL) salt

¼ tsp (1 mL) pepper

½ cup (125 mL) flour in a small bowl

3 Tbsp (45 mL) vegetable oil for frying

1 tsp (5 mL) Thai red curry paste

1 tsp (5 mL) minced garlic

1 2-oz (50 g) package of instant coconut cream powder or 1 can chilled coconut milk

2 Tbsp (30 mL) oyster sauce

2 Tbsp (30 mL) sugar

¼ cup (60 mL) smooth peanut butter

2 Tbsp (30 mL) chopped fresh cilantro or basil

Serves 4.

Per serving: 487 cals, 29.6 g fat, 6.1 g sat. fat, 92 mg cholesterol, 1130 mg sodium, 27.1 g carbs, 28.5 g protein

Best Ever Veggie Burgers

You can double this recipe; store patties in an airtight container and freeze them for up to 3 months. Thaw before reheating in the microwave.

½ lb (250 g) fresh mushrooms, diced

1 medium onion (about ½ lb [250 g]), diced

1½ cups (375 mL) unsalted, raw sunflower seeds

1¾ cup (185 mL) fresh, coarse breadcrumbs

½ cup (125 mL) finely chopped nuts, such as almonds, hazelnuts, Brazil nuts, or pistachios

2 large eggs

1 tsp (5 mL) garlic, minced

1 Tbsp (15 mL) Worcestershire sauce

1½ tsp (7.5 mL) salt

1 tsp (5 mL) pepper

1 Tbsp (15 mL) vegetable oil for baking sheet and skillet

Makes 7 substantial burger patties.

Per patty: 277 cals, 13.4 g fat, 1.7 g sat. fat, 60 mg cholesterol, 785 mg sodium, 28.6 g carbs, 10.7 g protein

Preheat the oven to 350°F (180°C) and oil a large non-stick skillet. Oil a baking sheet or line one with parchment paper.

Heat the oiled non-stick skillet on medium heat; add the mushrooms, garlic, and onions. Cook until the onion is transparent and the mushroom moisture evaporates, which will take about 7 to 10 minutes.

In a large bowl, combine the warm mushroom mix, sunflower seeds, breadcrumbs, and nuts. In a medium bowl, beat the eggs with the Worcestershire sauce and the seasonings. Add the eggs to the dry ingredients and mix well.

Place a 4-inch (10 cm) pastry ring or round cookie cutter in one corner of the baking sheet and sprinkle the inside of the ring with enough breadcrumbs to coat the bottom, about 1 tablespoon (15 mL). Add ⅓ cup (80 mL) of the seasoned mushroom mixture and pack it in evenly; sprinkle with 1 tablespoon (15 mL) of breadcrumbs. The resulting patty will be about ½ inch (1 cm) thick. Remove the ring and wipe it off. Continue making patties, evenly spacing them out on the baking sheet, until you have used up the filling; you should have 7 patties.

Bake patties for 20 to 25 minutes, or until firm to the touch and edges are light golden. Rotating the baking sheet once after 10 to 12 minutes of baking. If you are serving them immediately, remove from the baking sheet carefully because they are fragile when warm. If planning to reheat them, let them cool before removing from the baking sheet. Cover and refrigerate until 30 minutes before reheating or for up to 3 days, or wrap well and freeze for up to 2 months.

To reheat, wrap in foil and warm in a preheated 350°F (180°C) oven for 15 minutes, or microwave on medium for 2 to 3 minutes. (If topping with cheese, microwave on medium for 2 minutes before adding cheese and then microwave for 1 more minute to melt it.)

Serving Suggestion

Use Kaiser buns and top patties with grated Edam or Monterey Jack cheese, Basil Pesto (p. 94), Sun-dried Tomato Mayonnaise (p. 86), tomato slices, and lettuce.

Sun-dried Tomato Mayonnaise

For smooth mayo, this recipe requires a mini chopper or food processor. However, it can be made without one by finely chopping the tomatoes (the sauce will be a bit chunky but just as tasty).

2 Tbsp (30 mL) chopped sun-dried tomatoes, soaked in hot water for 15 minutes

1 cup (250 mL) mayonnaise, preferably Hellman's or Kraft Real Mayonnaise

Makes just over 1 cup (250 mL).

Per Tbsp (15 mL): 82 cals, 8.9 g fat, 0.9 g sat. fat, 4 mg cholesterol, 92 mg sodium, 0.2 g carbs, 0.2 g protein

Drain the tomatoes and place them in the processor bowl with ¼ cup (60 mL) mayonnaise. Process the mixture until smooth.

Empty it into a small bowl and stir in the remaining ¾ cup (185 mL) mayonnaise. Refrigerate, covered, for up to 2 weeks.

Coffee Rubbed New York Striploin Steaks with Hazelnut Sauce

Rich and robust with a hint of heat. Sensational! This recipe requires a coffee grinder or a mortar and pestle. Try with a creamy side such as Lemon Hazelnut Fettucine Alfredo (p. 96).

Use a coffee grinder or mortar and pestle to grind the peppercorns and coffee beans until some remain coarse and some are fully ground. Thinly coat the steaks with the mixture, using about 1 tablespoon (15 mL) per steak. Set aside on a plate for 30 minutes to bring to room temperature before grilling.

Lightly oil your grill and preheat it to 400°F (200°C).

In a medium skillet, melt the butter on medium heat. Add the shallots and cook them until transparent. Add the wine and continue cooking until the liquid reduces by half. (You can make the sauce to this point and then turn off the heat and cover and let sit for 30 to 60 minutes. To finish, uncover, turn heat to medium, and continue with the recipe.)

Add the stock and reduce the amount of liquid by half again. Whisk in the nut butter and salt.

Grill steaks to your liking, about 8 to 10 minutes in total for medium-rare, depending on the thickness. Let the steaks rest on a plate for 5 minutes before serving so they are juicier. They will continue to cook during this time. Drizzle each steak with warm Hazelnut Sauce before serving.

Steaks

2 Tbsp (30 mL) whole black peppercorns

2 Tbsp (30 mL) whole espresso beans or dark-roast coffee beans

4 8-oz (250 g) New York striploin steaks, preferably 1½-inch (4 cm) thick

vegetable oil for the grill

Hazelnut Sauce

2 Tbsp (30 mL) butter

2 shallots, minced

¼ cup (60 mL) dry white wine

½ cup (125 mL) beef stock

2 Tbsp (30 mL) hazelnut butter

¼ tsp (1 mL) salt

Serves 4.

Per steak with 2½ Tbsp (32 mL) sauce:
417 cals, 21.9 g fat, 8 g sat. fat, 152 mg cholesterol, 294 mg sodium, 4.4 g carbs, 50.3 g protein

Macadamia Madeira Pork Medallions

Pork tenderloin in a creamy, rich and seductive sauce! A crispy side such as Sweet Potato and Pecan Latkes (p. 97) is a good contrast.

1½ lb (750 g) pork tenderloin (2 small ones or 1 large one)

2 Tbsp (30 mL) butter

2 Tbsp (30 mL) Madeira from Portugal (found in the sherry section at the liquor store)

¼ cup (60 mL) macadamia nut butter

1 cup (250 mL) vegetable stock or chicken stock

½ tsp (2 mL) pepper

½ tsp (2 mL) salt

½ tsp (2 mL) garlic salt

Serves 4.

Per serving: 373 cals, 21.3 g fat, 6.6 g sat. fat, 124 mg cholesterol, 942 mg sodium, 6.7 mg carbs, 38.7 g protein

Preheat the oven to 350°F (180°C) and lightly oil a medium baking dish. Slice the pork tenderloin into ½-inch-thick (1 cm) medallions and sprinkle with ¼ teaspoon (1 mL) pepper.

Melt the butter in a large skillet on medium-high heat. Add the pork and cook for 3 to 4 minutes to brown them; flip and cook the other side for 3 to 4 minutes. Add the medallions to the baking dish and set aside.

Turn the heat to high and cook the juice in the skillet until it is dark brown, about 2 to 3 minutes. Add the Madeira to the skillet, which will steam up and sizzle a lot. Loosen any brown bits with a wooden spoon and cook until the skillet is dry and brown.

Add the vegetable stock and stir again to loosen any further brown bits from the bottom of the skillet. Add any meat drippings that have pooled in the baking dish to the stock mixture in the skillet.

Whisk in the nut butter; add the seasoning and mix well. Cook for a few minutes until sauce thickens to the consistency of gravy.

Pour sauce over the pork medallions and stir to coat. Cover and bake for 20 to 30 minutes to cook the pork through, checking for doneness after 20 minutes. (The pork should be firm to the touch and the juices will run clear.)

Macadamia Mahi-mahi with Tropical Salsa

The salsa for this dish can be prepared ahead of time, or while the fish is cooking. Serve this with Green Rice (p. 104) for a colourful dinner!

Fish

Salt and pepper the fillets, and then dredge them in flour to coat them well. One by one, dip the fillets in the beaten egg, letting any excess drip back into the bowl, before coating with the nuts. Refrigerate the fish, uncovered, for at least 30 minutes so the breading adheres.

Remove the fish from the fridge 30 minutes before baking to bring it to room temperature.

Preheat the oven to 375°F (190°C) and oil a baking sheet. Spray the tops of the fish fillets with vegetable oil before baking. Bake the fish until it is golden, cooked through, and firm to the touch, about 15 to 20 minutes. Cooking time may vary if the fish is thinner or thicker than 1½ inch (4 cm).

Salsa

Mix the mango, pineapple, green onions, lime juice, jalapeno, sugar, and seasoning. Let sit at room temperature to dissolve the sugar and salt and blend the flavours. Mix in the cilantro just before serving.

Serve fillets with salsa on the side.

Fish

4 6-oz (175 g) mahi-mahi fillets, 1½-inch (4 cm) thick, boneless and skinless

salt and pepper in shakers or grinders

½ cup (125 mL) flour, in a medium bowl

1 large egg, beaten, in a medium bowl

1 cup (250 mL) finely chopped macadamia nuts, in a medium bowl

vegetable oil spray

Salsa

1 mango, peeled and chopped into ½-inch (1 cm) cubes

½ a small pineapple, peeled, cored, and diced into ½-inch (1 cm) pieces

½ bunch green onions (about 3), trimmed and sliced ¼-inch (6 mm) thick

1 small jalapeno pepper, seeded and minced

2 Tbsp (30 mL) lime juice, preferably freshly squeezed

1 tsp (5 mL) sugar

¼ tsp (1 mL) salt

¼ tsp (1 mL) pepper

2 Tbsp (30 mL) minced fresh cilantro leaves

Serves 4.

Per 6-oz (175 g) fillet with ½ cup (125 mL) salsa: 521 cals, 28.6 g fat, 4.6 g sat. fat, 116 mg cholesterol, 202 mg sodium, 25.3 g carbs, 40.7 g protein

Poisson Almondine

This dish is an elegant classic with delicate lemon butter and toasted almonds. I recommend you serve it with Squash and Pecan Risotto (p. 105).

4 6-oz (175 g) boneless, skinless fish fillets, such as Pacific Grey Cod, Sablefish, or Halibut, ¾-inch (2 cm) thick

salt in a shaker

pepper in a mill or shaker

½ cup (125 mL) flour, in a medium bowl

4 Tbsp (60 mL) butter

½ cup (125 mL) dry white wine

2 Tbsp (30 mL) lemon juice

¼ cup (60 mL) toasted sliced blanched almonds

fresh lemon wedges for garnishing and squeezing on fish (optional)

Serves 4.

Per serving: 333 cals, 17.5 g fat, 7.8 g sat. fat, 94 mg cholesterol, 240 mg sodium, 10.3 g carbs, 33.5 g protein

Rinse and pat dry the fish fillets, and then salt and pepper them liberally. Dredge the fillets in flour, coating both sides well.

Heat a large, non-stick skillet on medium-high heat. Melt 2 tablespoons (30 mL) of butter until foaming; add the fish fillets, nice side down. Cook all 4 at once until golden brown, about 3 to 4 minutes. Add the remaining 2 tablespoons (30 mL) of butter. Carefully flip the fillets and cook until golden, 3 to 4 minutes more. Place the fillets on a plate and set aside.

Add the lemon juice and wine to the skillet. Boil the liquid for about 5 minutes until it is reduced to a third of the original volume. Return the fish to the pan with the sauce and cook for 1 to 2 minutes to heat through. (If the fish is thicker than specified, and not yet fully cooked in the middle, cover and simmer it for several minutes longer.) Fish should be firm to the touch and easily flake apart if pressed firmly.

Serve each fillet sprinkled with 1 tablespoon (15 mL) almonds and garnish with lemon wedges.

Rack of Lamb
with Honey Hazelnut Crust

For a wonderful fall/winter dinner, pair this dish with Mashed Potatoes with Blue Cheese and Walnuts (p. 100).

Preheat the oven to 400°F (200°C) and oil a large baking dish that can fit the two racks of lamb.

Mix the honey, mustard, seasoning, and rosemary together. Spread half of the mixture on the meaty side of each lamb rack. Mix the nuts and crumbs together. Completely cover the top of the racks with the crumb mix, using half on each one.

Spray the crumb-coated racks with vegetable oil to help them brown and place them in the baking dish.

Pour the wine into the bottom of the pan and roast the racks for about 20 minutes (for medium-rare), or longer if you prefer. Let racks cool 8 to 10 minutes before slicing.

Add ½ cup (125 mL) stock to the pan you used to cook the racks and stir to loosen any brown bits. If pan is stovetop-safe, heat it on a burner on medium-low (or transfer the juice to a medium sauce-pan). Add the mustard and the seasoning; whisk to mix. If the sauce is very scant, add a little more stock; mix well and heat through.

Slice the racks with one rib per slice to yield about 6 to 7 slices per rack. Drizzle with the mustard sauce and serve.

2 racks of lamb, at room temperature

2 Tbsp (30 mL) honey

2 Tbsp (30 mL) Dijon mustard

¼ tsp (1 mL) ground pepper

¼ tsp (1 mL) salt

1 tsp (5 mL) fresh rosemary leaves, minced

1 cup (250 mL) of toasted, rubbed hazelnuts, coarsely ground

1 cup (250 mL) Panko breadcrumbs or fresh white breadcrumbs

vegetable oil spray

½ cup (125 mL) dry white wine

2 Tbsp (30 mL) Dijon mustard

¼ tsp (1 mL) salt

¼ tsp (1 mL) pepper

½ to ¾ cup (125 to 185 mL) chicken stock or beef stock

Serves 4, with about 3 slices per person.

Per serving: 712 cals, 35.4 g fat, 6.4 g sat. fat, 152 mg cholesterol, 1298 mg sodium, 41.4 g carbs, 57 g protein

Veal Escalopes
with Mushroom Wine Sauce

A rich, velvety mushroom sauce that marries happily with Orzo with Balsamic Butter and Toasted Walnuts (p. 95).

1 recipe Almond Wine Sauce (p. 81)
1½ lb (750 g) veal leg slices, cut scaloppine style
freshly ground pepper from a grinder or shaker
1 cup (250 mL) beef stock
½ lb (250 g) fresh mushrooms, sliced
½ tsp (2 mL) minced garlic
3 to 4 Tbsp (45 to 60 mL) butter

Serves 6.

Per serving: 486 cals, 37.7 g fat, 20.6 g sat. fat, 192 mg cholesterol, 598 mg sodium, 9.2 g carbs, 27.9 g protein

Begin heating Almond Wine Sauce in a medium saucepan on medium-low heat.

Place the meat slices between sheets of wax paper. Use a flat-headed mallet to pound the meat to ¼-inch (6 mm) thickness. Pepper both sides of each slice and set aside.

In a medium-large skillet on medium-high heat, bring the stock to a boil. Add the mushrooms and cook for 4 to 5 minutes, stirring occasionally. Stir in the garlic. As mushrooms and garlic cook, the stock will reduce in volume. When there is very little stock remaining (only 2 to 3 tablespoons [30 to 45 mL]), add the mushroom mixture and remaining liquid to the Almond Wine Sauce and mix well.

In the empty skillet, melt 2 tablespoons (30 mL) butter on medium-high heat. Add the veal slices. Do not overlap the slices: fry them in 2 batches instead. Cook each side for 2 to 3 minutes, until lightly browned. Turn over and cook 1 to 2 minutes more; remove from pan and set aside. (If necessary, add the remaining butter to the skillet and fry the second batch.)

When the veal is done, drain or blot any excess butter remaining in the pan. Reduce the heat to medium-low and add the Mushroom Wine Sauce. Loosen any brown bits in the skillet and mix into the sauce. Add the veal, reheating it for 3 to 4 minutes before serving.

Side Dishes

Angel Hair Pasta with Basil Pesto

This delicate pasta gains a very bright flavour and colour when you add basil pesto.

In a small saucepan or skillet, melt the butter with the olive oil; add the Basil Pesto and mix well.

Have a large strainer with small holes ready in the sink. Bring a large pot of salted water to a boil. Cook the pasta according to package directions, stirring frequently at first to separate pasta strands, and then occasionally while cooking. It will only take 3 to 4 minutes of cooking for al dente. Drain the pasta well and place it back in the warm saucepan.

Mix the pesto with the warm pasta, pepper, and Parmesan. Serve immediately.

2 Tbsp (30 mL) butter

2 Tbsp (30 mL) olive oil

3 Tbsp (45 mL) Basil Pesto (p. 94)

1 Tbsp (15 mL) salt for pasta water

8 oz (250 g) dried capellini pasta (angel hair pasta)

½ tsp (2 mL) freshly ground pepper

¼ cup (60 mL) Parmesan cheese

Serves 4.

Per serving: 382 cals, 18.7 g fat, 6.3 g sat. fat, 21 mg cholesterol, 178 mg sodium, 43 g carbs, 10.4 g protein

Basil Pesto

For a traditional-style pesto, add ½ cup (125 mL) Parmesan cheese to this recipe. Use an ice cube tray to freeze small portions of this sauce, and then bag the cubes.

Place the herbs in a food processor, and drizzle with lemon juice and about half of the olive oil. Blend until the leaves are finely chopped, about 1 to 1½ minutes. Add the garlic, seasoning, and the nuts; blend again to finely chop the nuts. (The mixture should be fairly smooth but it won't be completely puréed.) Gradually add the remaining oil and blend until incorporated.

2 cups (500 mL) fresh parsley leaves, washed and dried and packed tightly

2 cups (500 mL) fresh basil leaves, washed and dried and packed tightly

2 Tbsp (30 mL) lemon juice, or white or red wine vinegar

1½ tsp (7.5 mL) minced garlic

½ cup (125 mL) olive oil

1 tsp (5 mL) salt

½ tsp (2.5 mL) pepper

½ cup (125 mL) toasted pine nuts (or substitute toasted walnuts, pecans, or hazelnuts)

Makes 2 cups (500 mL).

Per Tbsp: 45 cals, 4.5g fat, 0.7g sat fat, 76mg sodium, 0.6g carbs, 0.7g protein

Orzo with Balsamic Butter and Toasted Walnuts

This dish goes well with Veal Escalopes with Mushroom Wine Sauce (p. 92), or it makes an easy entree if you add sliced cooked meat (such as beef, pork, or chicken).

Have a large strainer with small holes ready in the sink. Bring a large pot of water, with 1 tablespoon (15 mL) of salt, to a boil. Add the pasta and boil it until tender, about 8 to 10 minutes. Drain and rinse well with hot water, shaking off any excess water.

Heat the oil, butter, and balsamic vinegar in a medium skillet or saucepan on medium heat. Add the pasta and stir well to coat it with the balsamic butter. Add the salt, pepper, and nuts; mix well. Serve immediately.

1 Tbsp (15 mL) salt for pasta water

1 cup (250 mL) dried orzo pasta

2 Tbsp (30 mL) walnut oil

2 Tbsp (30 mL) butter

1½ tsp (7.5 mL) balsamic vinegar

⅓ cup (80 mL) toasted, chopped walnuts

¼ tsp (1 mL) salt

¼ tsp (1 mL) freshly ground pepper

Serves 6.

Per serving: 228 cals, 12.7 g fat, 3.3 g sat. fat, 10 mg cholesterol, 3 mg sodium, 23 g carbs, 5.1 g protein

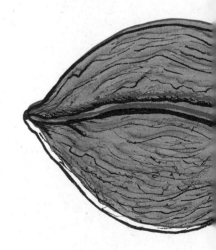

Lemon Hazelnut Fettuccine Alfredo

This rich, creamy pasta pairs well with Coffee Rubbed New York Striploin Steak with Hazelnut Sauce (p. 87).

Add 1 tablespoon (15 mL) salt to a large pot of water and bring it to a boil. Add the pasta, stirring frequently with a pasta fork, and cook according to the package directions for al dente, or to your liking, about 12 to 15 minutes.

While the pasta cooks, whisk the hot melted butter with the hazelnut butter in a small bowl. In a medium-large bowl, whisk the egg yolks into the hot whipping cream. Add the hazelnut-butter mixture, pepper, and lemon zest; mix well.

Drain the pasta and return it to the warm saucepan. Immediately add the sauce and toss to mix well. Top with the Parmesan cheese and chopped hazelnuts, and serve with the lemon wedges for squeezing over each serving. Serve immediately.

1 Tbsp (15 mL) salt for pasta water

8 oz (250 g) dried fettuccine pasta

3 Tbsp (45 mL) butter, melted for 1 minute on medium in the microwave just before adding

1 Tbsp (15 mL) hazelnut butter

2 large egg yolks, beaten, at room temperature

½ cup (125 mL) whipping cream, heated for 1 minute on medium in the microwave just before adding

¼ tsp (1 mL) pepper

zest of 1 lemon, minced
(cut lemon into wedges to serve on the side)

¼ cup (60 mL) Parmesan cheese

¼ cup (60 mL) toasted blanched hazelnuts, chopped

Serves 4.

Per serving: 528 cals, 32.2 g fat, 14.8 g sat. fat, 213 mg cholesterol, 137 mg sodium, 45.7 g carbs, 13.9 g protein

Sweet Potato and Pecan Latkes

Try these crispy latkes with Madeira Macadamia Pork Medallions (p. 88).

Preheat the oven to 250°F (120°C) to keep latkes warm while frying in batches.

In a large bowl, combine the two types of potatoes and the nuts. Add the flour and the seasonings; mix well. Stir in the egg white to coat the potato mixture well.

Add 1 inch (2.5 cm) of vegetable oil to a large, non-stick skillet; heat on medium-high heat until oil is rippling.

Add ⅓ cup (80 mL) portions to the hot oil, spaced 3 to 4 inches (8 to 10 cm) apart. Flatten then slightly to create latkes 3½ to 4 inches (9 to 10 cm) across, about ¼ inch (6 mm) thick. Cook for 1 to 2 minutes, until underside is golden; turn over. Brown the other side, about 1 to 2 minutes more.

Drain the cooked latkes on paper towels and keep warm in the oven while frying the remaining portions. Serve warm, with sour cream on the side if desired.

2 cups (500 mL) peeled and grated sweet potatoes

2 cups (500 mL) peeled and grated russet potatoes

¼ cup (60 mL) raw pecans, finely chopped

½ tsp (2 mL) pepper

½ tsp (2 mL) salt

¼ cup (60 mL) rice flour

1 egg white, lightly beaten

1 cup (250 mL) vegetable oil for frying

sour cream (optional)

Serves 6, with 2 latkes per person.

Per latke: 89 cals, 3 g fat, 0.2 g sat. fat, 113 mg sodium, 13.9 g carbs, 1.8 g protein

Cheddar Potatoes with Almond Crust

This dish is easier to make if the potatoes are cooked the day before so they are cold prior to slicing. Makes a great side dish for Cashew Glazed Salmon (p. 78).

8 medium-large red potatoes, scrubbed clean and poked with a fork for baking

vegetable oil

¼ cup (60 mL) butter

¼ cup (60 mL) flour

2 cups (500 mL) whole milk, heated to steaming in the microwave for 2 minutes on medium

½ tsp (2 mL) garlic salt

½ tsp (2 mL) pepper

½ tsp (2 mL) dry mustard powder

2 cups (500 mL) grated sharp or aged cheddar cheese

1 bunch green onions (about 6), trimmed and sliced into ¼-inch (6 mm) pieces

Preheat the oven to 400°F (200°C).

Dry and oil the potatoes and bake them in a large baking dish, uncovered, until tender though to the middle, about 35 to 45 minutes. Remove from the oven and cool completely. (You can cover and refrigerate them until you are ready to assemble this dish, up to 1 day ahead of time.)

Melt the butter in a medium saucepan on medium heat; add the flour and stir to blend. Add ⅔ cup (160 mL) of the hot milk, whisking until smooth. Add another ⅔ cup (160 mL) of milk, whisking well to prevent lumping. Cook for 5 to 8 minutes, or until the sauce thickens. Add the remaining milk and the seasoning.

Continue cooking the sauce, while whisking, until thick and smooth. Scrape the sides and bottom edge of the pan frequently and stir to incorporate any thick sauce. Add 1½ cups (375 mL) of the cheddar cheese and stir until thoroughly melted. Remove from heat and set aside.

Preheat the oven to 350°F and oil a large baking dish that can be used for both baking and serving.

Slice the baked potatoes into ⅓-inch (8 mm) thick rounds, discarding the very end pieces. Line the baking dish with half of the potato slices; top with half of the cheese sauce and sprinkle with half of the onions. Repeat with the remaining potatoes, sauce, and onions.

In a small bowl, mix together the almonds, crumbs, seasoning, parsley, and olive oil. Sprinkle the top of the baking dish with the remaining ½ cup (125 mL) cheese, and then cover it completely with the crumb mixture.

Bake for 30 to 40 minutes, or until bubbly and heated through.

⅓ cup (80 mL) ground almonds

⅔ cup (160 mL) Panko breadcrumbs

¼ tsp (1 mL) garlic salt

¼ tsp (1 mL) pepper

1 Tbsp (15 mL) dried parsley

3 Tbsp (45 mL) olive oil

Serves 15.

Per serving: 271 cals, 14.8 g fat, 7 g sat. fat, 30 mg cholesterol, 291 mg sodium, 25.4 g carbs, 9.1 g protein

Mashed Potatoes
with Blue Cheese and Walnuts

These rich, robust potatoes go well with Rack of Lamb with Honey Hazelnut Crust (p. 91). This dish can also be prepared ahead of time; add the nuts after reheating, just before serving.

3 lb (1.5 kg) russet potatoes, peeled and cut into 2-inch (5 cm) chunks

1 tsp (5 mL) salt

7 oz (200 g) blue cheese, crumbled and at room temperature

½ cup (125 mL) toasted walnuts, chopped coarsely

½ cup (125 mL) hot water

½ tsp (2 mL) pepper

salt, if needed (add cheese first, then taste)

Serves 8.

Per serving: 243 cals, 11.8 g fat, 5 g sat. fat, 18 mg cholesterol, 629 mg sodium, 25.5 g carbs, 8.4 g protein

Add the potatoes and salt to a large pot of water on high heat. Bring the water to a boil and cook the potatoes until very tender and easily broken apart when poked with a fork, about 10 to 15 minutes. Drain the potatoes well.

Add ½ cup (125 mL) hot water to the pot containing the potatoes. Mash well for about 2 minutes, and then whip the potatoes in a circular motion with the potato masher to cream them somewhat. If they are not very creamy and seem dry, add another 1 to 2 tablespoons (15 to 30 mL) hot water before mashing and mixing them 1 to 2 minutes more to produce smooth, creamy mashed potatoes.

Add the cheese and pepper to the pot, stirring to melt the cheese. Add the nuts. (If desired, hold back 1 to 2 tablespoons [15 to 30 mL] of the cheese and nuts for garnishing.) Taste mashed potatoes and add some salt if needed. Keep warm until serving.

Baked Red Potatoes
with Hazelnut Hollandaise

This elegant but easy-to-make recipe turns ordinary baked potatoes into something special.

Preheat the oven to 400°F (200 °C) and lightly oil a baking dish.

Poke each of the potatoes several times with a metal skewer or fork; rub enough olive oil on each potato to lightly coat the pierced skin. Place potatoes in the baking dish and sprinkle each one with a bit of coarse salt. Bake the potatoes until tender, about 40 to 50 minutes depending on the size of the potatoes.

Slice open the top of each potato and place a spoonful of Hazelnut Hollandaise in the middle. (The sauce recipe makes enough for 10 potatoes with 2 tablespoons [30 mL] of sauce each.) Serve with extra sauce on the side.

1 medium red potato per person, scrubbed and dried

olive oil

coarse sea salt

1 recipe Hazelnut Hollandaise (p. 6), at room temperature

Per potato with 2 Tbsp (30 mL) sauce: 309 cals, 22.2 g fat, 11.2 g sat. fat, 160 mg cholesterol, 425 mg sodium, 22.7 g carbs, 4.7 g protein

Barley Pilaf with Chestnuts

This dish goes well with hearty beef, bison, and lamb dishes, such as Glazed Bison Kebabs (p. 80), but it can also serve as a vegetarian entree if you use vegetable stock. This recipe requires some preparation in the morning, or the day before.

2 Tbsp (30 mL) butter

1½ cups (375 mL) diced onion (1 medium cooking onion)

¾ cup (185 mL) pearl barley

¼ tsp (1 mL) minced garlic

2¼ cups (560 mL) chicken stock

1 Tbsp (15 mL) dried parsley

¾ tsp (4 mL) salt

¼ tsp (1 mL) pepper

⅔ cup (160 mL) peeled and cooked chestnuts, chopped

1 cup (250 mL) sharp or aged cheddar cheese, grated

Serves 6.

Per serving: 272 cals, 12.1 g fat, 7.3 g sat. fat, 33 mg cholesterol, 697 mg sodium, 29.8 g carbs, 10.5 g protein

Oil a baking dish that can hold 4 to 5 cups (1 to 1.25 L) and which has a lid.

Melt the butter in a medium skillet on medium-high heat. Add the onion and cook until transparent, about 5 minutes. Add the barley and the garlic. Cook the barley mixture until light golden brown, about 8 to 10 minutes.

Remove from heat and place the mixture in the baking dish along with the chicken stock and seasoning. Cover and refrigerate for 8 hours or overnight. (This method softens the barley so it will absorb the stock.)

To finish, bring dish to room temperature, which will take 30 to 45 minutes. Preheat the oven to 375°F (190°C) and move a rack to the bottom third of the oven.

Bake barley, covered, for 60 minutes. Stir in the chestnuts; if there is any stock remaining, cook for 10 minutes more. Sprinkle the cheese over the pilaf and return dish to the oven for a few minutes to melt it. (You can also broil it for 1 to 2 minutes until bubbly, if you prefer.)

Mexican Rice Stuffed Peppers

These peppers go well with grilled fish, chicken, or steak but also work well as a vegetarian entree.

Preheat the oven to 375°F (190°C). Oil a medium-large baking dish that can fit 6 pepper halves without overlapping.

Slice the peppers in half from stem to base. Clean out the insides, removing and discarding the seeds and pith. Check that each one sits level with rounded side down. (If not, trim a minimal amount off the bottom but do not cut through the pepper.)

In a medium bowl, mix the rice, cheese, chilies, green onions, and seasonings.

In a small bowl, mix the breadcrumbs, ground almonds, olive oil, salt, and pepper.

Divide the rice mixture amongst the pepper halves and place them in the baking dish. Top each one with 2 tablespoons (30 mL) of the breadcrumb mixture, covering the rice completely.

Bake stuffed peppers for 45 minutes, or until the peppers are tender and the tops are golden. Serve with salsa on the side, if desired.

3 large bell peppers, any colour you like

Filling

1½ cups (375 mL) cooked rice, such as jasmine or basmati

1 cup (250 mL) grated sharp or aged cheddar cheese

½ of a small can of diced Mexican mild green chilies, about 3 Tbsp (45 mL)

½ bunch green onions (about 3), trimmed and chopped fine

½ tsp (2 mL) salt or seasoning salt

¼ tsp (1 mL) pepper

Topping

3 Tbsp (45 mL) coarse or Panko-style dry breadcrumbs

3 Tbsp (45 mL) ground almonds

2 Tbsp (30 mL) olive oil

¼ tsp (1 mL) salt

¼ tsp (1 mL) pepper

salsa (optional)

Serves 6.

Per serving: 246 cals, 14.6 g fat, 5.4 g sat. fat, 23 mg cholesterol, 479 mg sodium, 20.1 g carbs, 8.7 g protein

Green Rice

This colourful and flavourful rice variation combines nicely with the Macadamia Mahi-mahi (p. 89) for a very fresh-tasting dinner!

1 cup (250 mL) jasmine rice, rinsed three times in cold water

½ tsp (2 mL) salt

1 Tbsp (15 mL) butter

2 cups (500 mL) water

2 Tbsp (30 mL) minced fresh parsley leaves

¼ cup (60 mL) minced fresh cilantro leaves

¼ cup (60 mL) shelled pistachios, toasted and chopped

¼ cup (60 mL) pumpkin seeds, toasted

Serves 4.

Per serving: 294 cals, 11.4 g fat, 3.1 g sat. fat, 8 mg cholesterol, 69 mg sodium, 40.9 g carbs, 6.8 g protein

Place the rice in a medium saucepan. Mix in the salt and dots of the butter. Stir in the water and cover the pot. Heat on medium-high to a full boil. Keep boiling, gradually turning down the heat to prevent it from boiling over.

After 10 minutes, turn down the heat and simmer the rice for 10 minutes. Turn off the heat completely and let sit for 10 to 15 minutes.

Uncover and fluff the rice with a fork. Add the herbs, nuts, and seeds, mixing them in with a fork. Keep warm until serving.

Squash and Pecan Risotto

A perfect accompaniment to Pecan Coated Pork Chops with Tabasco Applesauce (p. 82).

In a medium-large, deep saucepan, melt the butter on medium-high heat. Cook the onion in the butter until transparent, about 5 minutes. Stir in the rice to brown it. After 5 minutes, the rice should be toasted and fragrant and the onions will be golden.

Add the wine. Stir constantly until almost all the liquid has been absorbed and then reduce the heat to medium.

Heat the stock separately, in a bowl in the microwave on medium-high heat for 2 minutes, or in a saucepan on medium heat until steaming (about 5 minutes).

Add 1 cup (250 mL) of hot stock to the pot with the rice. Stir again and cook until the liquid is almost all absorbed. Repeat this procedure, stirring the risotto and adding 1 cup (250 mL) of stock at a time, for about 20 to 30 minutes. Once all the liquid has been added, continue stirring frequently to prevent sticking, and cook the risotto until it becomes creamy and has the consistency of porridge.

Stir in the squash, heating it through before adding the seasoning. Just before serving, stir in the Parmesan, parsley, and pecans.

3 Tbsp (45 mL) butter

1 medium onion, diced

1½ cups (375 mL) Arborio or another risotto rice

½ cup (125 mL) dry white wine

6 cups (1.5 L) low-sodium vegetable or chicken stock

1 tsp (5 mL) salt

½ tsp (2 mL) pepper

2 cups (500 mL) squash, cooked and then cubed

½ cup (125 mL) grated Parmesan cheese

2 Tbsp (30 mL) minced fresh parsley leaves

½ cup (125 mL) toasted pecans, chopped

Serves 6.

Per serving: 375 cals, 16.3 g fat, 6.1 g sat. fat, 24 mg cholesterol, 682 mg sodium, 45.3 g carbs, 11.9 g protein

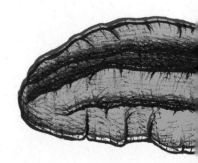

Roasted Asparagus Prosciutto Bundles

Beautiful bunches with robust flavour and a mouthwatering sauce.

24 pencil-thick asparagus stalks (about 1lb [500 g]), ends snapped off

3 thin slices of prosciutto (Italian cold-smoked ham), 3 inches (8 cm) wide and 8 to 10 inches (20 to 25 cm) long

salt and pepper in shakers or grinders

2 Tbsp (30 mL) balsamic vinegar

¾ cup (185 mL) Hazelnut Hollandaise (p. 6)

Serves 4.

Per bundle with 2½ Tbsp (37.5 mL) sauce:
372 cals, 32.8 g fat, 16.7 g sat. fat, 255 mg cholesterol, 1189 mg sodium, 7.2 g carbs, 11.8 g protein

Preheat the oven to 350°F (180°C) and oil a shallow, medium baking dish. Trim the ends of the asparagus to an even length.

Heat a large pot of water to boiling and prepare a large bowl of cold water. Add the asparagus to the pot and cook for 1 minute only. Remove and dunk in cold water immediately to stop the cooking.

Assemble 4 groups of asparagus (6 pieces per group), with the heads all at one end. Roll 1 piece of prosciutto around each group and place seam down in the baking dish. (You can prepare the dish to this point, cover, and refrigerate until later; just bring the bundles to room temperature before baking.)

Salt and pepper the bundles and drizzle with the vinegar. Bake for 15 to 20 minutes to cook the prosciutto and heat the asparagus through. While they are baking, reheat Hazelnut Hollandaise.

To serve, spoon 2 to 3 tablespoons (30 to 45 mL) warm Hazelnut Hollandaise over the middle of each bundle.

Green Beans
with Lemon and Walnuts

Fresh, light and easy!

Bring a large pot of water to a full boil; add the beans. Cook small beans for 1 minute; medium beans for 2 minutes; and large bean for 3 minutes. Drain and rinse with cold water to stop the cooking.

In a large skillet, melt the butter on medium heat. Add the beans and gently toss them in the butter to coat them well. Season with the salt and pepper. Stir frequently while you heat them through. This will take 4 to 5 minutes.

Add the lemon and thyme; mix well. Cook for 1 to 2 minutes more. Add the walnuts, mix well, and serve.

1 lb (500 g) green beans, stem ends snipped off and discarded

3 Tbsp (45 mL) butter

¼ tsp (1 mL) salt

¼ tsp (1 mL) freshly ground pepper

zest of 1 lemon

1 tsp (5 mL) minced fresh thyme leaves

¼ cup (60 mL) toasted walnut pieces, chopped

Serves 4.

Per serving: 173 cals, 13.3 g fat, 5.8 g sat. fat, 23 mg cholesterol, 156 mg sodium, 9.8 g carbs, 3.3 g protein

Grilled Corn with Spicy Pecan Butter

A fun version of corn on the cob for your next barbecue. You can prepare the spiced honey butter 1 to 2 days ahead: cover and refrigerate; bring to room temperature to serve.

2 Tbsp (30 mL) honey

½ cup (125 mL) butter, at room temperature

½ tsp (2 mL) ground cinnamon

¼ tsp (1 mL) ground ginger

¼ tsp (1 mL) cayenne pepper

½ tsp (2 mL) salt

2 tsp (10 mL) salt for the corn water

8 large cobs of corn, preferably a sweet variety such as peaches and cream, shucked

vegetable oil spray or 2 Tbsp (30 mL) vegetable oil, to rub on corn

¼ cup (60 mL) toasted pecans, finely chopped and on a plate for rolling the corn in

Serves 8.

Per cob: 273 cals, 16.5 g fat, 7.7 g sat. fat, 31 mg cholesterol, 166 mg sodium, 27 g carbs; 4.1 g protein

Mix the honey with the butter and spices until smooth. Set aside.

Preheat the barbecue grill on high.

Add 2 teaspoons (10 mL) salt to a large pot of water and bring to a boil. Add the corn and boil for 7 to 8 minutes, until tender. With a clean tea towel or paper towel, dry off the hot, cooked corn and then oil it lightly.

Grill the corn on high heat for 2 to 3 minutes per side to add distinct grill marks. Remove the cobs from the grill and spread each one with 1 tablespoon (15 mL) of spiced butter before rolling it in the toasted nuts. Serve immediately.

Cooking Tip:

If the honey is cold or too thick, microwave it on medium-low heat for 30 to 60 seconds to liquify it.

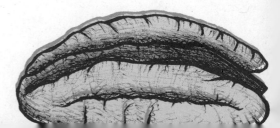

Roasted Brussels Sprouts with Sherry Walnut Glaze

This version will convince those who aren't excited about Brussels sprouts to become loyal fans.

Fill the bottom of a large steamer with 4 inches of water and pre-heat it on medium-high heat. (If you don't have a steamer, fill a large, deep, stainless-steel skillet with a lid with 1 cup [250 mL] of water.)

If the sprouts vary in size, cut the larger ones in half to have a consistent size. Steam the sprouts until tender, about 15 minutes. (If your steamer cannot hold all the sprouts, steam them in 2 batches.) Check for doneness: they should be cooked through when poked with a skewer or knife. Set aside.

In a large, non-stick skillet, heat the walnut oil on medium and brown the walnuts for 5 minutes. Remove from heat and set aside.

Heat 2 tablespoons (30 mL) of the olive oil in a large, non-stick skillet on medium heat and fry the shallots until transparent, about 5 minutes. Add the garlic, vinegar, mustard, and seasoning; whisk in the remaining olive oil.

Gently stir in the cooked sprouts. Add the walnuts, including any walnut oil from the pan, and coat the sprouts well. Cook the mixture until heated through, about 10 minutes, stirring frequently.

3 lb (1.5 kg) of young Brussels sprouts, stems trimmed

½ cup (125 mL) chopped shallots (3 medium-large ones)

1 tsp (5 mL) minced garlic

¼ cup (60 mL) sherry vinegar or white balsamic vinegar

3 Tbsp (45 mL) Dijon mustard

⅓ cup (80 mL) olive oil

½ tsp (2 mL) salt

½ tsp (2 mL) pepper

2 Tbsp (30 mL) walnut oil (or substitute olive oil)

½ cup (125 mL) walnut halves, coarsely chopped

Serves 10.

Per serving: 213 cals, 14.4 g fat, 1.6 g sat. fat, 257 mg sodium, 14.6 g carbs, 6 g protein

Spaghetti Squash
with Browned Butter and Walnuts

This sauce also pairs well with other vegetables, or use it for pasta.

3 lb (1.5 kg) spaghetti squash

½ cup (125 mL) butter

½ cup (125 mL) walnuts, coarsely chopped

3 Tbsp (45 mL) dry white wine

1½ tsp (2 mL) lemon juice

¼ tsp (1 mL) pepper

1 Tbsp (15 mL) chopped fresh herbs (such as thyme leaves, sage, oregano, tarragon, or parsley)

Serves 8.

Per serving: 181 cals, 16.3 g fat, 7.6 g sat. fat, 31 mg cholesterol, 200 mg sodium, 6.5 g carbs, 1.7 g protein

Preheat the oven to 350°F (180°C) and oil a large baking pan.

Use a large knife to split the squash in two from stem to end. Remove the seeds and stringy centre and discard.

Place squash halves cut side down in a 1- to 2-inch (2.5 to 5 cm) deep baking dish. Add ½ cup (125 mL) of water. Bake in the bottom third of the oven for 20 minutes.

Check for doneness by scraping at the insides of the squash with a dinner fork. Squash is ready when the flesh easily pulls off in thin spaghetti-like strands. If it is not done yet, bake for another 10 minutes and try again.

Once squash has cooled off, use a fork to remove the cooked flesh from each half until only a ¼ inch (6 mm) layer remains, then switch to a spoon. Discard the empty squash shell or use one half (the nicest one) to serve the squash in. The squash can be cooked and shredded a day or two ahead if refrigerated; frozen spaghetti squash flesh lasts for 3 months if wrapped well (thaw before reheating).

Reheat squash in a covered dish in the microwave on medium high, 2 minutes for 1 cup (250 mL) of squash (no need to add water).

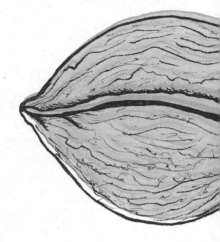

Heat ¼ cup (60 mL) butter in a skillet on medium-high heat; add the walnuts. Cook until they are golden and the butter starts to brown, about 5 minutes. Transfer the nuts to a plate but leave the butter in the skillet. Add the wine and increase the heat to high. Bring the mixture to a boil and boil for 2 to 3 minutes to reduce the volume to ¼ cup (60 mL). Reduce heat to low and add the herbs and pepper. Whisk in the remaining butter, 1 tablespoon (15 mL) at a time, whisking well after each addition. Stir in the nuts.

Add the nut–butter mixture to the hot squash; stirring well to coat. Top the squash with the fresh herbs and serve immediately.

Beets with Red Wine Glaze and Toasted Hazelnuts

A delicious, gourmet way to prepare beets!

8 medium beets or 4 large ones (2 lb [1 kg]), trimmed of greens and scrubbed but not peeled or cut

2 cups (500 mL) dry red wine

¼ tsp (1 mL) salt

¼ tsp (1 mL) pepper

2 Tbsp (30 mL) butter

½ cup (125 mL) toasted blanched hazelnuts, coarsely chopped

Serves 8.

Per serving: 126 cals, 7.6 g fat, 2.1 g sat. fat, 8 mg cholesterol, 162 mg sodium, 11.9 g carbs, 2.7 g protein

Cook the whole beets in boiling water until tender through to the centre, which will 25 to 30 minutes if they are large ones, or 18 to 20 minutes for medium ones. Drain them and let cool completely before handling.

To avoid beet stains, wear plastic gloves or place plastic bags over your hands. Rub the peels off the beets, which should come off easily when you pull down on the skin. Halve medium beets or quarter large ones.

Heat the wine in a medium-large skillet on medium-high heat. Boil the wine until it is reduced to a quarter of the original volume, or ½ cup (125 mL) in total; this will take about 15 minutes. Add the seasoning and mix well.

Add the beets and stir to coat them with sauce. Cook until the beets are glazed and heated through, about 5 to 7 minutes.

Add the butter and mix well. Place beets in a serving dish and sprinkle with the toasted hazelnuts.

Orange Hazelnut Carrots

This is a simple, tasty dish that both children and adults enjoy.

Cut the carrots on an angle into ½-inch (1 cm) slices.

Add the slices to a medium pot, cover with water and bring to a boil. Boil carrots until they are tender when poked by a fork or skewer, which will take about 10 to 15 minutes.

In a small saucepan, melt the butter on medium-low heat. Mix in the juice concentrate and seasoning; heat for 1 to 2 minutes. Remove sauce from heat and set aside.

Drain the carrots well. Add the orange butter and nuts; stir to coat well.

1 lb (500 g) medium carrots, peeled and trimmed

2 Tbsp (30 mL) butter

2 Tbsp (30 mL) frozen orange juice concentrate, thawed

¼ tsp (1 mL) salt

¼ tsp (1 mL) pepper

¼ cup (60 mL) toasted blanched hazelnuts, chopped

Serves 4.

Per serving: 168 cals, 10.5 g fat, 3.9 g sat. fat, 16 mg cholesterol, 188 mg sodium, 16.1 g carbs, 2.4 g protein

Almond Parmesan Parsnips

An interesting way to introduce parsnips to children or those undecided adults.

1½ lb (750 g) parsnips (approximately 3 medium)
½ cup (125 mL) flour
3 Tbsp (45 mL) grated Parmesan cheese
3 Tbsp (45 mL) ground almonds
¼ tsp (1 mL) pepper
vegetable oil spray

Serves 6.

Per serving: 169 cals, 3.7 g fat, 0.9 g sat. fat, 2 mg cholesterol, 69 mg sodium, 29.3 g carbs, 4.7 g protein

Preheat the oven to 400°F (200°C) and thoroughly oil a shallow baking dish or baking sheet. Peel the parsnips and cut into 2½- to 3-inch (6 to 8 cm) lengths. Quarter the parsnips vertically through the core; trim off and discard any woody centres.

Combine the flour, cheese, almonds, and pepper in a medium bowl; mix well.

Heat a medium pot of water to boiling. Blanch the parsnips until tender when poked with a fork, about 1 to 2 minutes. Drain them somewhat.

While parsnips are still wet, toss them in the flour mixture. (The parsnips can be prepared to this point and covered and refrigerated for 1 day. Just bring them to room temperature before baking.)

Spray the tops and sides of the parsnips with oil. Bake them for 20 to 30 minutes, or until golden and caramelized.

Roasted Squash
with Mushrooms and Hazelnuts

Well suited to a fall or winter dinner with roasted meat or poultry. You can use any orange-flesh squash, such as pumpkin, or butternut or acorn squash. Try this recipe with wild mushrooms for an interesting twist!

Preheat the oven to 400°F (200°C) with the rack in the middle of the oven.

Place the squash cubes and shallots in a large baking dish. Cut medium mushrooms in half or quarter large ones; add them to pan. Drizzle the vegetables with the olive oil, stirring them as you add the oil. Sprinkle them with the salt, pepper, and thyme; mix well.

Roast the vegetables for 20 to 30 minutes, stirring every 10 minutes. Check halfway through cooking for dryness. If the juice is reducing too quickly, drop the heat to 375°F (190°C). In the last 5 to 8 minutes of cooking, add the nuts. Cook until the vegetables have golden edges and the mushroom juice has evaporated.

3 cups (750 mL) squash, cut into 1½-inch (4 cm) cubes

12 medium shallots, peeled and left whole or in segments

12 large white mushrooms (or 24 medium)

¼ cup (60 mL) olive oil

1 Tbsp (15 mL) fresh thyme leaves, chopped (or substitute 1½ tsp [7.5 mL] dried thyme)

½ tsp (2 mL) garlic salt

¼ tsp (1 mL) pepper

½ cup (125 mL) toasted blanched hazelnuts

Serves 8.

Per serving: 145 cals, 11.6 g fat, 1.2 g sat. fat, 151 mg sodium, 7.4 g carbs, 2.8 g protein

Zucchini Ribbons
with Pistachio Lime Butter

Prep the zucchini ahead of time for a quick side dish that goes well with grilled or roasted meat, poultry, fish, or seafood.

2 medium zucchini
1 Tbsp (15 mL) olive oil for sautéeing
1 Tbsp (15 mL) lime juice
3 Tbsp (45 mL) butter
¼ tsp (1 mL) pepper
¼ cup (60 mL) pistachios, toasted and chopped

Serves 4.

Per serving: 176 cals, 16.2 g fat, 6.5 g sat. fat, 23 mg cholesterol, 90 mg sodium, 4.4 g carbs, 3.4 g protein

Hold the zucchini vertically. Using a vegetable peeler, slice down one side of the zucchini in the same spot repeatedly. Peel that side until you reach the white seedy centre then stop and rotate to next side. Continue peeling until you have made thin ribbons from 4 sides of the zucchini. Prepare the second zucchini in the same way. You will have the ribbons for the recipe plus two centres (soft and square-shaped) remaining, which can be diced and added to soup or grated for use in cake or muffins. Ribbons can be prepared earlier in the day, and then covered and refrigerated until you are ready to cook them.

In a small saucepan, heat the lime juice on medium heat and cook it for 1 to 2 minutes to reduce it in volume to only 1 teaspoon (5 mL) of liquid remaining. Turn the heat to low and gradually whisk in the butter followed by the pepper.

In a medium skillet, heat the olive oil on medium-high heat. Sauté the zucchini ribbons for 1 to 2 minutes to heat through but barely cook them. Remove from heat.

Add the lime butter and the nuts; mix well and serve immediately.

Decadent Desserts and Sweet Treats

Brie and Walnut Stuffed Figs

This is a very easy and elegant dessert. I think it's an excellent choice for a special occasion fall dinner.

1 4-oz (125 g) wheel Brie cheese

12 large fresh figs (such as California-grown brown Turkey figs or a local green variety)

½ cup (125 mL) toasted walnut pieces

¼ cup (60 mL) honey

2 Tbsp (30 mL) brandy or orange-flavoured brandy

Serves 6, with 2 figs per person.

Per serving: 267 cals, 10.5 g fat, 3.2 g sat. fat, 14 mg cholesterol, 91 mg sodium, 38 g carbs, 5.3 g protein

Preheat the oven to 350°F (180°C) and oil a medium baking dish that can hold all 12 figs.

Carefully trim the rind off the Brie without wasting any of the soft cheese inside; discard the rind. Mix the soft cheese with ¼ cup (60 mL) of the walnuts.

With your index finger, make a hole in the bottom of each fig and push the flesh to the sides from the middle, leaving the outside intact. The space inside each fig should accommodate about 1 tablespoon (15 mL) of the Brie mixture. Stuff each fig with a piece of cheese and sit it upright (cheese side down) in the baking dish.

Whisk the honey with the brandy and drizzle it over the figs. Roast the figs for about 15 minutes, until the cheese is melted and the sauce is bubbly.

To serve, put two figs on each plate, drizzle with sauce from the pan, and sprinkle with the remaining nuts. Serve immediately.

Coffee Cashew Crème Brûlée

An interesting variation on a classic favourite.

Custard

Preheat the oven to 350°F (180°C) and fill a deep baking dish that can hold all 6 ramekins without them touching with 2 inches (5 cm) of water.

In a small bowl, dissolve the coffee in the rum and vanilla.

In a medium saucepan, heat the whipping cream, milk, and white sugar on medium heat to steaming, about 5 to 7 minutes. Once the sugar is dissolved, add the coffee mixture and the chocolate. Stir until the chocolate is melted and the mixture is smooth, about 1 to 2 minutes. Do not allow to boil.

Pour the hot cream into the egg yolks and whisk well to incorporate. Divide the mixture among the ramekins. Bake for 30 minutes until the tops are set.

Topping

While the custards are baking, mix the brown sugar, espresso, and cashew pieces together.

After the custards have been in the oven for 30 minutes, remove and add 1½ to 2 tablespoons (22.5 to 30 mL) of topping. Bake the custards until the sugar begins bubbling, another 10 to 15 minutes. Cool and refrigerate until serving.

Custard

1½ tsp (2 mL) instant coffee powder or granules
½ tsp (2 mL) vanilla
2 tsp (10 mL) dark rum
1 ⅓ cups (330 mL) whipping cream
⅔ cup (160 mL) milk
2 Tbsp plus 2 tsp (40 mL) white sugar
4 oz (125 g) white chocolate, chopped
7 large egg yolks in a large bowl, slightly beaten

Topping

⅓ cup (80 mL) packed brown sugar
1 Tbsp (15 mL) finely ground espresso
⅓ cup (80 mL) toasted cashews, chopped

Serves 6.

Per serving: 537 cals, 39.2 g fat, 21 g sat. fat, 527 mg cholesterol, 73 mg sodium, 35.6 g carbs, 10.2 g protein

Cooking Tip:

The 7 egg whites not needed for this recipe can be frozen in an airtight container for up to 3 months and used in other recipes that require only egg whites.

Chocolate Caramel Pecan Bread Pudding

This is the ultimate comfort food! Try it topped with whipped cream or ice cream, and drizzled with some chocolate or caramel sauce.

4 cups (1 L) 1-inch (2.5 cm) chocolate cake cubes (made from brownies, muffins, loaf, or cake)

12 1-inch (2.5 cm) caramels, preferably Kraft brand, wrappings removed and cut into 8 pieces each

⅓ cup (80 mL) chocolate chips or chopped semi-sweet dark chocolate

⅓ cup (80 mL) toasted, chopped pecans

1 cup (250 mL) 2% or whole milk

1 cup (250 mL) light cream

⅓ cup (80 mL) chocolate sauce

3 large eggs and 2 large egg yolks, in a large bowl, at room temperature

⅓ cup (80 mL) sugar

½ tsp vanilla

½ tsp cinnamon

Serves 6.

Per serving: 583 cals, 31.6 g fat, 12.3 g sat. fat, 384 mg cholesterol, 326 mg sodium, 62.6 g carbs, 12.7 g protein

Preheat the oven to 375°F (190°C) and oil six 3-inch (8 cm) ramekins or a 2- to 3-quart (2 to 3 L) baking dish.

Divide half of the cake pieces amongst the ramekins or layer the bottom of the baking dish. Top the cake layer with half of the chocolate, caramel pieces, and pecans. Repeat layering, beginning with the cake.

Heat the milk, cream, and chocolate sauce in a medium saucepan on medium heat until just steaming but not boiling, about 5 to 7 minutes.

In a large bowl, whisk together the eggs, yolks, sugar, vanilla, and cinnamon. Whisk the hot cream into the egg mixture and mix well. Pour the egg mixture over the cake layers; gently press down on the top layer until the liquid is absorbed. Place ramekins or baking dish on a baking sheet to catch any drips in the oven. Bake 3-inch (8 cm) ramekins for 20 minutes and a large baking dish 30 to 45 minutes. Check middle for doneness; a toothpick should come out clean. If not done, return it to the oven for 5 more minutes. This dish is best served warm.

Honey Roasted Pears
with Praline Sauce

A great fruit dessert that tastes rich but which is amazingly light.

Preheat the oven to 400°F (200°C) and oil a medium baking dish that will hold all 6 pear halves.

Peel the pears before slicing them in half from stem to end. Scoop out the core and stem from each half using a melon baller. Coat the pear halves with the lemon juice, shaking off any excess before placing them in the baking dish.

Drizzle each pear half with 1 tablespoon (15 mL) of honey and 1 teaspoon (5 mL) of melted butter. Bake the pears until tender, about 20 minutes, basting the halves several times with juice from the pan. Top each half with a scoop of ice cream, a drizzle of Praline Sauce, and a sprinkle of toasted almonds. Serve immediately.

3 large pears, medium-firm ripeness (Bartletts or Anjous are recommended)

2 to 3 Tbsp (30 to 45 mL) lemon juice to coat the pears to prevent browning

⅓ cup (80 mL) honey

2 Tbsp (30 mL) melted butter

¾ cup (185 mL) Praline Sauce (p. 122), warmed in a small saucepan on low heat for 5 to 10 minutes

3 cups (750 mL) vanilla ice cream

2 Tbsp (30 mL) toasted sliced or slivered blanched almonds for garnishing

Serves 6, with half a pear and ½ cup (125 mL) ice cream per person.

Per serving: 320 cals, 9.2 g fat, 4.6 g sat. fat, 23 mg cholesterol, 26 mg sodium, 57.4 g carbs, 1.8 g protein

Praline Sauce

This dairy-free sauce is silky smooth and delicious—it tastes like it was made with cream.

1 cup (250 mL) sugar
1 tsp (5 mL) lemon juice
¾ cup (185 mL) Reduced Almond Milk (p. 122)

Makes 1 cup (250 mL).

Per Tbsp (15 mL): 53 cals, 0.3 g fat, 12.5 g carbs

In a medium saucepan on high heat, melt the sugar with the lemon juice and 1 tablespoon water. Bring the sugar to a rapid boil and cook the sugar for 10 to 15 minutes to caramelize it. Watch it closely as it starts to turn golden; it can burn easily at this stage.

When then sugar is a deep golden colour, remove pot from heat and immediately add the Reduced Almond Milk. The mixture will bubble up so be ready with a whisk and stir the sauce until smooth.

Keep warm on low heat if using right away, or cool, cover, and refrigerate for up to 5 days.

4 cups (1 L) almond milk, preferably Almond Breeze "Original"

Makes about 1½ cups (375 mL).

Per Tbsp (15 mL): 4 cals, 0.4 g fat

Reduced Almond Milk

Bring the milk to a boil in a large pot on medium-high heat. Boil the milk for 20 to 25 minutes to reduce it but not scorch it, whisking occasionally to incorporate any thick milk that accumulates on the sides of the saucepan. You can reduce the heat slightly during this time but keep it at a full boil. You should end up with a thicker almond "cream." (This mixture will look slightly granular but will be smooth in recipes. Cool, cover, and refrigerate until needed.)

Reduced milk will last the same amount of time as an opened carton of regular almond milk (check the "best before date").

Sautéed Pineapple
with Kahlua Pecan Sauce

Yum!!!

In a small saucepan on medium heat, melt the first six ingredients together. Cook the sauce until the sugar dissolves, about 3 to 5 minutes. Keep Kahlua Pecan Sauce warm, or make ahead and reheat just before serving in a small saucepan on low heat.

Slice the pineapple crosswise into 6 equally thick rounds.

Spray a large nonstick skillet liberally with oil and heat to medium high. Sauté the pineapple slices until light golden, about 3 to 4 minutes per side.

Add the pecans to the sauce just before serving. Portion out 2 tablespoons (30 mL) Kahlua Pecan Sauce per slice of pineapple and top with ½ cup (125 mL) ice cream.

2 Tbsp (30 mL) butter
1 Tbsp (15 mL) lemon juice
½ cup (125 mL) brown sugar
1 Tbsp (15 mL) Kahlua liqueur
1 Tbsp (15 mL) brandy
1 tsp (5 mL) vanilla
1 whole cored and peeled fresh pineapple
vegetable oil spray for the skillet
⅓ cup (80 mL) toasted pecans, chopped
3 cups (750 mL) vanilla ice cream

Serves 6.

Per serving (with sauce and ice cream): 263 cals, 11.8 g fat, 4.8 g sat. fat, 23 mg cholesterol, 32 mg sodium, 37.1 g carbs, 1.8 g protein

Almond Cheesecake with Praline Sauce

Prepare a day ahead of time for all those cheesecake and/or almond lovers.

Base
Preheat the oven to 350°F (180°C).

Mix the cookie crumbs with the sugar. Stir in the melted butter; mix well. Press mixture into a 9-inch (23 cm) springform pan, reaching 1 inch (2.5 cm) up the sides. Pack the crumbs in very tightly so the base will come out in one piece.

Filling
Beat the cream cheese in the bowl of a stand mixer with a paddle attachment until smooth. (This step can also be done with a hand-held mixer.)

In a medium bowl, whisk the sugar with the eggs and flavourings. Add the egg mixture to the cream cheese and beat until smooth. Scrape down the sides of the bowl frequently to incorporate all of the cream cheese. You want the mixture to be completely smooth.

Pour the cream cheese filling over the crust and bake on the middle rack of the oven for 30 minutes. Rotate the pan 180 degrees and bake for another 30 minutes.

Cool to room temperature before covering and refrigerating overnight.

Base

1 cup (250 mL) graham cracker crumbs

3 Tbsp (45 mL) ground almonds

3 Tbsp (45 mL) sugar

3 Tbsp (45 mL) melted butter

Filling

4 8-oz (250 g) packages regular cream cheese, at room temperature

1¼ cup (310 mL) sugar

5 large eggs, at room temperature

2 Tbsp (30 mL) Amaretto liqueur

½ tsp (2 mL) vanilla

½ tsp (2 mL) almond extract

Cooking Tip:

Make sure the cream cheese is very soft to avoid lumps in your cake. If needed, unwrap and microwave, uncovered on a plate, on low heat until very soft, about 1 to 2 minutes.

Topping

Remove the cake from the pan by running a knife around the inside edge before releasing the latch. (If you want to move the cake from the springform base, place a lifter between the cake and the pan base. Sweep the lifter in a circular motion around the pan's base to release the crust.) Slide the cake onto a platter and slice with a warmed knife for clean cuts.

Sprinkle with the toasted almonds and serve with Praline Sauce on the side or drizzled overtop of individual servings.

Topping

1 recipe Praline Sauce (p. 122)

¾ cup (185 mL) toasted slivered or sliced blanched almonds

Serves 10.

Per serving, with 1½ Tbsp (22.5 mL) sauce: 637 cals, 38.4 g fat, 18.8 g sat. fat, 189 mg cholesterol, 286 mg sodium, 61 g carbs, 11.7 g protein

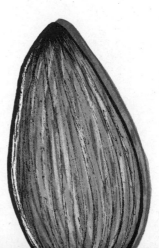

Peanut Butter Banana Cream Pie

This is a fun and child-friendly version of an old classic.

10-inch (25 cm) purchased pie shell, baked
according to package directions and cooled

Custard Filling

¼ cup (60 mL) cornstarch

¾ cup (185 mL) sugar

3 cups (750 mL) 2% or whole milk

1 tsp (5 mL) vanilla

1 Tbsp (15 mL) dark rum

1 tsp (5 mL) unflavoured gelatin

4 large egg yolks

Cooking Tip:

To speed up the cooling/setting process when
you make the custard, place the warm custard
in a medium-large bowl and then put the bowl
into an ice-water bath (a large bowl filled half-full
with ice water). Stir the custard with a whisk
occasionally to incorporate the thickened custard
on the sides of the bowl. The mixture will set in
about 15 to 20 minutes using this method.

Custard Filling

In a medium bowl, mix the cornstarch with the sugar. In a medium saucepan, bring 2½ cups (625 mL) milk, the vanilla, and the rum to a boil. Whisk half of the hot milk mixture (about 1½ cups [375 mL]) into the sugar and cornstarch before adding it to the pot. Cook on medium-low, whisking until thickened.

Whisk the gelatin into ½ cup (125 mL) milk, let sit for 2 to 3 minutes to soften, but not more than 5 minutes or it will set. Add the gelatin–milk mixture to the hot filling, mixing well to melt it into the custard.

In a separate bowl, whisk the yolks; add a quarter of the hot filling mixture to the bowl and blend well. Add the yolk mixture to the pot, along with any remaining hot milk, and cook, stirring continuously. Do not let the custard come to a boil but cook it until it thickens enough to coat the back of a spoon, about 8 to 10 minutes. Stir frequently while cooking. Remove from heat and cool.

Lay plastic wrap on the surface of the filling and refrigerate until set, about 3 hours.

Peanut Butter Banana Layer

Spread the pie shell with the peanut butter and sprinkle with ¼ cup (60 mL) of peanuts. Add a ¼-inch (6 mm) thick layer of sliced bananas. Cover the bananas with the cold custard and cover with plastic wrap. Chill for at least 1 hour to set the pie.

Topping

In a large bowl, whip the cream, icing sugar, and vanilla until firm peaks form. Evenly distribute whipped cream overtop of the pie and sprinkle with 2 tablespoons (30 mL) of peanuts. Keep pie refrigerated under serving time.

Peanut Butter Banana Layer

¼ cup (60 mL) smooth peanut butter

¼ cup (60 mL) toasted unsalted peanuts

3 large ripe but firm bananas,
sliced ¼ inch (6 mm) thick

Topping

2 cups (500 mL) whipping cream

⅓ cup (80 mL) icing sugar

½ tsp (2 mL) vanilla

2 Tbsp toasted unsalted peanuts

Serves 8.

Per serving: 629 cals, 40.2 g fat, 18.6 g sat. fat, 187 mg cholesterol, 216 mg sodium, 55.6 g carbs, 10.9 g protein

Maple Pecan Pumpkin Pie

This recipe has the power to convert the non-pumpkin-pie people into pumpkin lovers! It is best when the pie is baked the day before and the whipped cream is added the next day.

10-inch (25 cm) unbaked deep-dish pie shell

Filling

3 large eggs

¾ cup plus 1 Tbsp (200 mL) white corn syrup

¾ tsp (4 mL) ground cinnamon

½ tsp (2 mL) ground ginger

¼ tsp (1 mL) ground nutmeg

¼ tsp (1 mL) salt

2 Tbsp (30 mL) flour

1¼ cups (310 mL) light cream

1 14-oz (398 mL) can (or 1¾ cups [435 mL]) pumpkin purée

½ cup (125 mL) toasted pecans, chopped

Maple Whipped Cream

2 cups (500 mL) whipping cream

¼ cup (60 mL) maple syrup

1½ Tbsp (22.5 mL) icing sugar

¼ tsp (1 mL) maple flavouring, preferably Mapeleine

¼ cup (60 mL) toasted pecans, chopped

Serves 8.

Per serving: 620 cals, 41 g fat, 18.6 g sat. fat, 171 mg cholesterol, 323 mg sodium, 55.1 g carbs, 7.7 g protein

Preheat the oven to 375°F (190°C) with a rack placed in the bottom third of the oven.

Filling

In a large bowl, beat the eggs and the corn syrup together.

Sift the dry ingredients into a small bowl. Add about ¼ cup (60 mL) of the cream; whisk until smooth. Whisk this paste into the egg mixture until smooth. Gradually add the pumpkin and the rest of the cream, whisking until smooth. Pour the filling into the pie shell and sprinkle with ½ cup (125 mL) pecans.

Bake until the centre is set, about 1 hour. If the crust starts getting too brown, cover it with some foil until the filling is done. Cool completely and refrigerate, preferably all day or overnight.

Maple Whipped Cream

Place all the ingredients in a large bowl and whisk the mixture until firm peaks form, stopping occasionally to scrape the sides of the bowl. (You can also do this in a large, deep bowl using a hand mixer.) Top the pie with the whipped cream piled high and sprinkle the top with ¼ cup (60 mL) pecans.

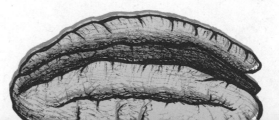

Coffee Pecan Torte

A light cake sandwiched together with a rich cream that tastes like a latte.

Cake

Preheat the oven to 350°F (180°C), with a rack placed in the bottom third of the oven. Line an 8-inch (20 cm) springform pan with parchment paper; butter and flour the pan.

Using a mixer with a whisk attachment, beat the yolks with the sugar. Transfer the yolk mixture to a large bowl and wash the bowl you just used. In the clean bowl, whisk the egg whites and cream of tartar until stiff peaks form, about 4 to 5 minutes on high speed. Fold the whites into the yolks and then gradually fold in the nuts, breadcrumbs, and flour.

Scrape the batter into the prepared pan and bake for 45 minutes. When cake is done, the top should spring back when pressed. Cool completely before turning out of the pan.

Coffee Cream

In a large bowl, beat the cream with the sugar and 2 tablespoons (30 mL) of the Kahlua. Beat the cream until soft peaks form, about 4 to 5 minutes. Scrape down the sides of the bowl and continue to beat until stiff peaks appear, about 1 minute more.

Assembly

Using a bread knife, slice the cake horizontally into 3 1-inch (2.5 cm) thick layers. Sprinkle the insides of the layers with the remaining 2 tablespoons (30 mL) of Kahlua. Use half the Coffee Cream to coat the cake's bottom and middle layers. Place the bottom cake layer, topped with filling, in the middle of a large plate. Centre the middle layer, also topped with filling, on top of it. Add the final layer (the one without any filling). Ice the exterior of the cake with the remaining Coffee Cream. Chill for 1 to 2 hours before serving.

Cake

6 large eggs, separated and at room temperature

¾ cup (185 mL) sugar

½ tsp (2 mL) cream of tartar

¾ cup (185 mL) ground pecans

⅓ cup (80 mL) dry breadcrumbs

¼ cup (60 mL) flour, sifted

Coffee Cream

2 cups (500 mL) whipping cream

1 Tbsp (15 mL) sugar

¼ cup (60 mL) Kahlua liqueur

Serves 8.

Per serving: 469 cals, 32.4 g fat, 15 g sat. fat, 236 mg cholesterol, 108 mg sodium, 36.4 g carbs, 7.7 g protein

Chocolate Almond Fudge Cake

This is a very easy chocolate cake that gets rave reviews from all.

1 cup (250 mL) flour

¼ cup plus 2 Tbsp (90 mL) unsweetened dark Dutch cocoa powder

½ tsp (2 mL) baking soda

¼ tsp (1 mL) salt

½ cup plus 2 Tbsp (155 mL) toasted blanched almonds, chopped

½ cup (125 mL) melted butter

1¼ cup (60 mL) golden brown sugar

2 large eggs, beaten

1 tsp (5 mL) vanilla

½ cup (125 mL) hot water

1 recipe Chocolate Almond Ganache (p. 131)

Serves 8.

Per serving: 491 cals, 20.4 g fat, 13.3 g sat. fat, 84 mg cholesterol, 259 mg sodium, 68.7 g carbs, 8.3 g protein

Preheat the oven to 350°F (180°C). Butter and line an 8-inch (20 cm) round cake pan with parchment paper, and then butter the parchment.

In a medium bowl, sift the dry ingredients and stir in ½ cup (125 mL) chopped almonds.

In a large bowl, mix the butter and brown sugar together with a wooden spoon. Mix in the eggs and vanilla. Add the dry ingredients and stir until combined. Add the hot water; mix until smooth. Pour the batter into the prepared pan and place in the middle of the oven.

Bake for 40 minutes and then test for doneness: a toothpick should come out clean. If not done yet, bake for a maximum of 5 minutes more and retest for doneness. Do not overbake.

Cool for 15 to 20 minutes, and then run a knife around the inside edge of the pan. Invert gently to turn the cake out of the pan. Cool cake completely before removing the parchment and placing onto a serving plate.

Slowly pour one third to one half of the Chocolate Almond Ganache over the cake. With a palette or spreader knife, distribute the mixture over the top and down the sides to coat them well. Pour the rest of the ganache over the cake, spreading it mostly to cover the top but also letting some dribble down the sides. To garnish, sprinkle the top of the cake with the remaining 2 tablespoons (30 mL) of chopped almonds.

Chocolate Almond Ganache

This chocolate ganache is dairy-free but you would never know it! When you melt it, this ganache also works well as a fudge sauce for ice cream.

In a medium saucepan, bring the Reduced Almond Milk, vanilla, and rum to a boil. Turn off the heat and add the chocolate. Cover and let rest for 5 minutes to melt the chocolate; whisk until smooth.

If using as a spreadable icing, cover and chill; bring ganache to room temperature before icing. If using as a cake glaze, cool until somewhat thickened before pouring over the cake.

1 cup (250 mL) Reduced Almond Milk (p. 122)

1 tsp (5 mL) vanilla

1 Tbsp (15 mL) dark rum

8 oz (250 g) semi-sweet dark chocolate, chopped into ¼-inch (6 mm) pieces

Makes 2 cups (500 mL).

Per Tbsp (15 mL): 40 cals, 2.1 g fat, 4.7 g carbs, 0.5 g protein

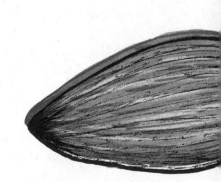

Red Velvet Chocolate Tarte

The "red" in this recipe refers to red wine, which marries very well with dark chocolate and intensifies the chocolate flavour. Note: this recipe requires a food processor for making the crust and a 9-inch (23 cm) French tarte pan.

Crust

Preheat the oven to 375°F (190°C).

In a food processor, chop the nuts finely; add the sugar and process to combine. Drizzle in the melted butter and pulse a few times before turning the crumbs out into the tarte pan. Press the crumb mixture into the edges of the pan and up the sides to form a shell. Smooth the upper edge and even out any thicker areas. Use the back of a serving spoon to firmly press the crumbs and pack them in tightly. Bake it for 10 minutes, until golden brown. Cool completely and then chill while making the filling.

Filling

Heat the whipping cream, sour cream, wine, and sugar in a medium-large saucepan on medium-high heat. Bring the mixture to a boil and cook for 1 to 2 minutes to dissolve the sugar; whisk to mix well.

Remove from heat and immediately add the chocolate and cover. Let sit for 5 minutes to thoroughly melt the chocolate, and then whisk until smooth. As it is cooling, whisk occasionally to prevent a skin from forming on top.

Cool filling for 5 to 10 minutes before pouring into the chilled tarte shell and garnishing with pecans (finely spaced so there will be 1 per wedge when sliced). Chill this magnificent tarte for several hours until the chocolate filling is set.

Crust
2 cups (500 mL) raw pecans
½ cup (125 mL) sugar
3 Tbsp (45 mL) melted butter

Filling
½ cup (125 mL) whipping cream
⅓ cup (80 mL) sour cream
½ cup (125 mL) dry red wine
13 oz (400 g) semi-sweet dark chocolate, chopped into ¼-inch (6 mm) pieces

Garnish
8 whole toasted pecans

Serves 8.

Per serving: 631 cals, 45.2 g fat, 16.7 g sat. fat, 35 mg cholesterol, 14 mg sodium, 49.8 g carbs, 6.1 g protein

Decadent Chocolate Pudding with Chestnut Cream

The chestnut cream adds a unique finish to this delicious comfort food. (The cream also works well as a filling for sponge cake.)

Ready six 3-inch (8 cm) ramekins or custard cups.

In a medium saucepan, heat the milk with the flavourings and bring it to a boil. Remove from heat and add the chocolate, stirring until melted and combined.

Pour the hot chocolate mixture into the egg yolks and whisk until smooth. Drop the heat to low and scrape the mixture back into the saucepan. Return the pan to the burner and cook, stirring constantly, until thickened. Do not allow pudding to boil or it may curdle! Remove from heat and portion the pudding into the ramekins to cool.

Cool completely; cover and refrigerate for at least 1 hour before serving.

Using a stand mixer, or a bowl and a hand mixer, whisk the chestnut purée with the rum and half of the whipping cream until smooth. Add the icing sugar and the remaining whipping cream; whisk until soft peaks form, about 4 to 5 minutes. Continue whisking, carefully, until stiff peaks form, about another minute. Be careful not to overmix or the cream will curdle.

Top each pudding portion with ⅓ cup (80 mL) Chestnut Cream.

1 cup (250 mL) whole milk

1 Tbsp (15 mL) dark rum

½ tsp (2 mL) vanilla

6 oz (175 g) semi-sweet chocolate, such as Baker's or Lindt, chopped

6 large egg yolks in a medium bowl, slightly beaten

2 Tbsp (30 mL) sweetened chestnut purée

1½ tsp (2 mL) dark rum

1 cup (250 mL) whipping cream

2 Tbsp (30 mL) icing sugar

Serves 6.

Per serving (with cream): 438 cals, 32.4 g fat, 17.1 g sat. fat, 447 mg cholesterol, 50 mg sodium, 27.8 g carbs, 9.2 g protein

Cooking Tip:

Extra egg whites can be used in many different desserts, such as angel food cake, meringues, and macaroons. They can also be combined with whole eggs for scrambling or making omelettes.

Double Chocolate Pecan Brownies

Delicious, moist brownies with intense chocolate flavour.

5 oz (150 g) unsweetened chocolate, chopped in ¼-inch (6 mm) pieces

½ cup (125 mL) butter

3 large eggs

¾ cup (185 mL) white sugar

1 cup (250 mL) packed dark brown sugar, preferably Best Brown Sugar brand

1 tsp (5 mL) vanilla

1¼ cups (60 mL) toasted chopped pecans

1¼ cups (60 mL) flour

1 Tbsp (15 mL) vegetable oil

1 cup (250 mL) semi-sweet chocolate chips

Makes 24.

Per brownie: 270 cals, 15.3 g fat, 6.5 g sat. fat, 36 mg cholesterol, 15 mg sodium, 29.7 g carbs, 3.3 g protein

Preheat the oven to 350°F (180°C) and line a large, rectangular baking pan with parchment paper.

Melt the butter and the unsweetened chocolate in a bowl in the microwave on medium heat for 2 minutes. Stir the chocolate several times and cook for 1 to 2 more minutes, until completely melted. Cool the chocolate mixture to room temperature.

In a medium-large bowl, beat the eggs, sugars, and vanilla. Stir in the chocolate mixture and ¾ cup (185 mL) pecans. Gradually add the flour, stirring with a wooden spoon or spatula until just mixed. Stir in the oil and chocolate chips until just blended; do not overmix.

Spread the batter evenly in the lined pan and sprinkle with remaining ½ cup (125 mL) pecans. Gently press the nuts into the batter and bake for 20 to 25 minutes. Brownies are perfectly cooked when a toothpick comes out clean except for clinging crumbs. Cool completely before cutting into 24 pieces. Store (or freeze) brownies in an airtight container.

Nanaimo Bars

My version of Nanaimo, British Columbia's famous bar. This recipe doubles well and freezes well.

Base

Oil a large, rectangular baking pan.

In a large saucepan on medium heat, melt the butter with the sugar and cocoa; mix well. Stir in the eggs and the vanilla. Cook for 1 to 2 minutes until the mixture thickens. Remove from heat and add the graham cracker crumbs, coconut, and nuts; mix thoroughly.

Press the mixture into the pan, evenly distributing it into the corners and packing it in tightly. Cover and refrigerate.

Icing

In a medium bowl, gradually add the sugar to the butter and mix with a wooden spoon until smooth. Stir in the vanilla and mix well. Spread the icing evenly over the base. Cover the pan and return to the fridge to chill.

Topping

Melt the chocolate chips with the butter in a bowl in the microwave on medium-low heat for 2 minutes. Remove and stir for 1 to 2 minutes to see if the chocolate is completely melted. If there are still chunks of chocolate, cook for 30 more seconds and stir again. Repeat as needed until the chocolate chips are all melted. Spread the chocolate thinly over the icing layer, coating the top well. Refrigerate again until the chocolate is set but still soft enough that you can score lines in it. Cut into 48 bars.

Base

1 cup (250 mL) butter

½ cup (125 mL) sugar

⅔ cup (160 mL) unsweetened dark Dutch cocoa powder, sifted

2 large eggs, beaten

2 tsp (10 mL) vanilla

2 cups (500 mL) graham cracker crumbs

2 cups (500 mL) unsweetened medium grated coconut

¾ cup (185 mL) toasted pecans, chopped

Icing

½ cup (125 mL) butter, at room temperature

2 cups (500 mL) icing sugar, sifted

½ tsp (2 mL) vanilla

Topping

1⅓ cups (330 mL) semi-sweet chocolate chips

2 Tbsp (30 mL) butter

Makes 48 bars.

Per bar: 165 cals, 11.1 g fat, 6.2 g sat. fat, 26 mg cholesterol, 25 mg sodium, 15.4 g carbs, 1.4 g protein

Luscious Lemon Bars

These bars are rich and creamy but have a light and refreshing taste. They also freeze well.

Base

1 cup (250 mL) butter

½ cup (125 mL) icing sugar, sifted

2 cups (500 mL) flour

1 large egg

zest from one lemon, minced

Cream Cheese Layer

⅓ cup (80 mL) spreadable cream cheese

Topping

½ cup (125 mL) butter

2½ cups (625 mL) icing sugar, sifted

2 Tbsp (30 mL) lemon juice

½ cup (125 mL) toasted sliced blanched almonds

Makes 48 triangular bars.

Per bar: 117 cals, 7.4 g fat, 4.1 g sat. fat, 22 mg cholesterol, 7 mg sodium, 11.9 g carbs, 1.1 g protein

Cooking Tip:

If you are doubling this recipe, use only 1 egg not 2. The egg is added to make the crust less crumbly but too much egg makes for a tough crust.

Base

Preheat the oven to 325°F (160°C) and oil a large rectangular baking pan.

In a medium bowl, cream the butter and the icing sugar together. Mix in the egg and gradually add the flour. Press the mixture evenly into the pan. Bake for 20 to 25 minutes; the edges should be golden when it's done. Cool completely.

Cream Cheese Layer

Spread the cream cheese over the shortbread base to coat it completely but thinly.

Topping

In a medium-large bowl, mix the butter with half of the icing sugar using a wooden spoon before incorporating the lemon juice. Gradually add the remaining icing sugar and mix until smooth. Top the cream cheese layer evenly with the lemon icing before sprinkling it with the almonds. Gently press the nuts into the icing to secure them. Cover and chill before slicing. Cut into 4 rows along the long side of the pan and 6 rows along the short side; then slice pieces in half on the diagonal.

Buttery Walnut Slice

This is one of those sinfully rich treats that goes well with coffee and tea.

Preheat the oven to 400°F (200°C) and oil a medium, square baking pan.

Base

In a medium bowl, cut the butter into the flour using a pastry blender or rub it in by hand to form a crumble with shortbread consistency. Press the mixture firmly into the prepared pan. Bake for 10 minutes, until partially set but not browned.

Filling

Drop the oven temperature to 350°F (180°C). In a medium bowl, whisk the eggs with the sugar. Stir in the flour, salt, and baking powder; mix well. Add the coconut and walnuts. Spread the mixture over the base. Bake for 20 minutes until lightly browned and the filling is set. Cool completely.

Icing

Using a wooden spoon, cream the butter in a medium bowl while gradually adding the icing sugar. Mix in the vanilla and spread the icing over the walnut layer. Chill to set the icing before slicing into 32 pieces.

Base

½ cup (125 mL) butter, chopped

1 cup (250 mL) flour

vegetable oil for the baking pan

Filling

2 large eggs

1¼ cup (60 mL) brown sugar

2 Tbsp (30 mL) flour

⅛ tsp (0.5 mL) salt

½ tsp (2 mL) baking powder, sifted

½ cup (125 mL) unsweetened medium grated coconut

1 cup (250 mL) toasted walnuts, chopped

Icing

¼ cup (60 mL) butter, at room temperature

1 cup (250 mL) icing sugar, sifted

½ tsp (2 mL) vanilla

Makes 32 bars.

Per bar: 137 cals, 7.2 g fat, 3.3 g sat. fat, 25 mg cholesterol, 17 mg sodium, 16.3 g carbs, 1.4 g protein

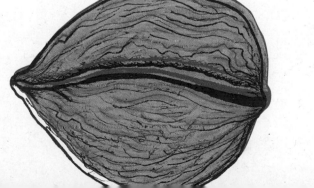

Mexican Wedding Cookies

These are seriously the best cookies on the planet!

Preheat the oven to 350°F (180°C) and lightly oil several large baking sheets.

In a large bowl, cream the butter and sugar together using a wooden spoon before beating in the egg yolk. Add the orange zest and vanilla; mix well. Gradually add the flour and then the nuts; incorporate thoroughly.

Press the dough into 2 logs approximately 8 inches (20 cm) long, 2 inches (5 cm) wide, and 1 inch (2.5 cm) high, with rounded corners. Slice each log into 24 pieces, about ⅓-inch (8 mm) thick. Press each rectangle to a ¼-inch (6 mm) thickness.

Space the cookies 2 inches (5 cm) apart and bake until the edges are golden, about 16 to 20 minutes. (If baking two batches of cookies at the same time, switch which racks the pans are on halfway through the baking.)

Cool cookies for at least 10 minutes to firm them up, and then dip each one into the icing sugar to liberally coat both sides.

1⅛ cup (280 mL) butter

¾ cup (185 mL) sugar

1 large egg yolk

1 Tbsp (15 mL) orange zest

1 tsp (5 mL) vanilla

2 cups (500 mL) flour

½ cup (125 mL) blanched almonds, finely chopped

½ cup (125 mL) pecans, finely chopped

1 cup (250 mL) icing sugar, sifted, for dusting cookies after baking

Makes 4 dozen cookies.

Per cookie: 100 cals, 6.2 g fat, 3 g sat. fat, 20 mg cholesterol, 1 mg sodium, 10.1 g carbs, 1 g protein

Cooking Tip:

These cookies freeze well but leave the icing sugar step until after you thaw them.

Chocolate Almond Drops

These crispy, crunchy chocolate treats are perfect at Christmas time. The recipe doubles well and freezes well.

Preheat the oven to 325°F (160°C).

In a large bowl, cream the butter and sugar together with a wooden spoon. Stir in the flour and cocoa until well incorporated. Add the almonds and mix into a dough. Chill for 30 minutes if too soft to handle.

Roll the dough into 1-inch (2.5 cm) balls and place on ungreased baking sheets. Bake for 20 minutes. Cool for several minutes before rolling the cookies in the icing sugar to coat them well.

½ cup (125 mL) butter

3 Tbsp (45 mL) icing sugar, sifted

⅔ cup (160 mL) flour

⅓ cup (80 mL) unsweetened dark Dutch cocoa powder, sifted

1 cup (250 mL) finely chopped almonds

1 cup (250 mL) icing sugar, sifted, for coating warm cookies

Makes 36 cookies.

Per cookie: 65 cals, 4.8 g fat, 1.9 g sat. fat, 7 mg cholesterol, 4.4 g carbs, 1 g protein

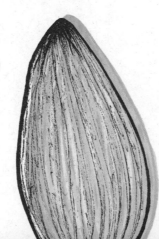

Doug's Breakfast Cookies

This cookie is the perfect breakfast food for my husband, Doug, because it is hearty and portable for commuting. Just one holds him until lunchtime! The recipe is great for using up those small amounts of nuts and dried fruit in your pantry. Chocolate chips can be added to the cooled batter if desired. The cookies also freeze well when stacked in a plastic container.

Preheat the oven to 350°F (180°C) and line 3 large baking sheets with parchment paper.

Mix the oats, fruit, wheat germ, seeds, coconut, and nuts in a large bowl. Melt the butter in a large saucepan with the sugar, honey, hot water, seasoning, and vanilla. Mix well and cook over medium heat until the sugar is fully melted, about 3 to 5 minutes. Remove from heat and add the dry ingredients to it gradually, mixing well. (If you want to add chocolate, let the mixture cool completely first.)

½ cup (125 mL) butter

¾ cup (185 mL) dark brown sugar (not demerara)

½ cup (125 mL) honey

¼ cup (60 mL) hot water

1 tsp (5 mL) salt

½ tsp (2 mL) cinnamon

2 tsp (10 mL) vanilla

3 cups (750 mL) large-flake old-fashioned oats

1½ cups (375 mL) dried cranberries

⅓ cup (80 mL) toasted wheat germ or oat bran

⅓ cup (80 mL) toasted sesame seeds

⅓ cup (80 mL) sunflower seeds

½ cup (125 mL) pumpkin seeds

½ cup (125 mL) unsweetened medium grated coconut

4 cups (1 L) variety of chopped nuts (almonds, walnuts, pecans, hazelnuts, peanuts, cashews, etc.)

1½ cups (375 mL) chocolate chips (optional)

Makes 36.

Per cookie: 298 cals, 15.7 g fat, 4.9 g sat. fat, 7 mg cholesterol, 70 mg sodium, 32.9 g carbs, 6.9 g protein

Portion out ⅓ cup (80 mL) of batter for each 3-inch (8 cm) cookie, with about 8 per baking sheet. Wet your fingers with cold water to prevent them from sticking to the mixture. Press the batter into even circles with smooth edges and make the cookies ⅓-inch (8 mm) thick.

Bake cookies for 15 to 16 minutes, or less if making smaller cookies. Rotate the baking sheets halfway through the baking time. The cookies should be medium gold in colour around the edges. Cool completely before trying to move them (they need to set first or they will break). If you are short on pans, slide the parchment (with the cookies on it) onto the counter to cool.

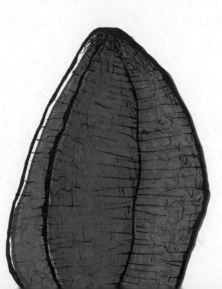

Cooking Tip:

You can use any amount of nuts, seeds, and fruit that totals 7½ cups (1.875 L). You can also bake this mixture as a granola: Use 3 large, oiled baking sheets to spread it out on and stir every 5 minutes while baking. (Makes 24 cups [6 L] with the chocolate chips added after baking.)

Almond Shortbread

My mom used to make these cookies every Christmas. Now I do and they're my family's favourite! This recipe also doubles well and freezes well.

1 cup (250 mL) butter, at room temperature
½ cup (125 mL) sugar
1½ cups (375 mL) flour
1 cup (250 mL) ground blanched almonds
1 cup (250 mL) granulated sugar, for coating warm cookies

Makes 4 dozen medium cookies.

Per cookie: 88 cals, 5.4 g fat, 2.6 g sat. fat, 10 mg cholesterol, 1 mg sodium, 8.8 g carbs, 1 g protein

Preheat the oven to 325°F (160°C).

In a large bowl, cream the butter and sugar together with a wooden spoon. Slowly add the flour and mix well. Add the nuts gradually, mixing well to incorporate them.

Roll out the dough to ¼-inch (6 mm) thickness and cut out 2- × 3-inch (5 × 8 cm) shapes using cookie cutters. (If they stick a bit, dip them in some flour.)

Bake on ungreased baking sheets until light golden around the edges, about 12 to 15 minutes. Cool for several minutes before coating both sides of each slightly warm cookie with sugar.

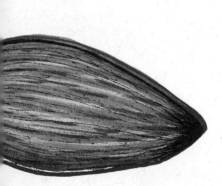

Pecan Shortbread

The brown sugar gives these shortbread cookies a caramel flavour that goes well with the pecans. This recipe doubles well and freezes well.

Preheat the oven to 350°F (180°C) and lightly oil 2 baking sheets.

In a large bowl, cream the butter and the sugar with a wooden spoon; mix in the salt and pecans. Gradually add the flour, mixing well. Form the dough into a ball, wrap in plastic wrap, and refrigerate for 30 minutes.

Roll out about half of the dough to ¼-inch (6 mm) thickness and use cookie cutters to create 2- × 3-inch (5 × 8 cm) shapes. Repeat until all the dough is used up.

Bake cookies until lightly browned, about 12 to 15 minutes.

1 cup (250 mL) butter, at room temperature
½ cup (125 mL) packed brown sugar
⅛ tsp (0.5 mL) salt
½ cup (125 mL) ground pecans
2 cups (500 mL) flour

Makes 48 medium cookies.

Per cookie: 62 cals, 4.7 g fat, 2.5 g sat. fat, 10 mg cholesterol, 7 mg sodium, 4.2 g carbs, 0.6 g protein

Brazil Nut Stuffed Dates

These dates are probably the easiest dipped candy ever made and the dried fruit goes great with the dark chocolate. They also freeze well.

24 whole dates, pitted

24 Brazil nuts

8 oz (250 g) dark-chocolate dipping wafers

Makes 2 dozen.

Per confection: 199 cals, 8.4 g fat, 3.1 g sat. fat, 2 mg sodium, 28.2 g carbs, 2.5 g protein

Line a baking sheet with parchment paper.

Slit the dates with a small paring knife and insert one Brazil nut into the centre of each date. Press the date around the Brazil nut to seal it shut.

Melt half the chocolate in the microwave on medium-low heat for 2 minutes. Stir and repeat for 1 minute at a time until completely melted.

Use a fork to pick up each date and dip it in the melted chocolate. Coat the date well, and then drop it onto the parchment. Using the end of a small spoon, fill any holes in the date from the fork with some melted chocolate. (Melt more chocolate for dipping as needed.)

Allow the chocolate on the confections to harden before serving or storing, which will take about 1 hour in a cool place. (You can refrigerate them to reduce the setting time to about 30 minutes.) Store them in an airtight container for up to 3 days.

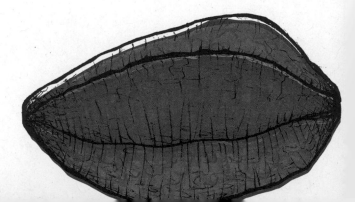

Brazil Nut Toffee

Trust me, this recipe is worth all the stirring!

Cover a medium baking sheet with foil and oil it liberally (or line with parchment paper).

Melt the butter in large, heavy saucepan on medium-high heat. Add the rest of ingredients, except the nuts, and bring the mixture to a boil. Continue boiling, stirring constantly, for 20 minutes.

Test the mixture by dropping a little bit into a cup of ice water; it should form into a hard, crunchy ball. (If you have a candy thermometer, it should reach 302°F [150°C].) If the candy has not reached the "hard crack" stage, continue to cook and stir, retesting every 3 to 5 minutes until done.

Stir in the nuts and pour the toffee onto the baking sheet to harden. You may have to spread the mixture into the corners of the baking sheet and evenly distribute it. When toffee is half-set but still impressionable, after about 20 to 30 minutes, use a knife to score it into 1-inch squares (10 rows across and 15 rows down). When toffee has completely cooled and hardened after about 1½ to 2 hours, snap the toffee into pieces and store in an airtight container.

1 cup (250 mL) butter

3 cups (750 mL) brown sugar

1 cup (250 mL) corn syrup

1 10-oz (300 mL) can sweetened condensed milk, preferably Eagle Brand

1 cup (250 mL) toasted Brazil nuts, coarsely chopped

Makes 150 pieces.

Per square: 50 cals, 2 g fat, 1.1 g sat. fat, 4 mg cholesterol, 8 mg sodium, 7.5 g carbs, 0.3 g protein

Almond Brittle

Very addictive. Makes a fun gift if you can bear to part with it!

Cover a medium baking sheet with parchment paper or oiled foil.

In a large, heavy, non-stick skillet on medium heat, combine the butter, corn syrup, and sugar. Cook until melted and bubbling, about 5 minutes, stirring frequently.

Add the almonds and continue cooking for another 5 to 10 minutes, until the nuts are browned and the sugar is completely caramelized to a deep golden-coloured liquid. Stir frequently for even browning.

Spread the mixture over the pan and sprinkle with the salt. Cool on a rack until hard, and then break into chunks.

¼ cup (60 mL) butter
¼ cup (60 mL) corn syrup
1⅓ cups (330 mL) sugar
2 cups (500 mL) whole blanched almonds
¼ tsp (1 mL) salt

Makes 3 cups (750 mL).

Per ¼ cup (60 mL): 296 cals, 16.5 g fat, 3.6 g sat. fat, 10 mg cholesterol, 60 mg sodium, 31.9 g carbs, 4.9 g protein

Chocolate Hazelnut Truffles

Sinfully delicious! You can make these truffles ahead of time and freeze them for up to 3 months.

Melt the chocolate in a double boiler on low heat. Remove from heat and cool to room temperature.

Using a wooden spoon, beat the egg yolks with the butter, rum, and coffee in a medium-large bowl. Add the melted chocolate in small amounts and beat until shiny. Cover bowl with plastic wrap and chill until hard.

With a melon baller, or a small teaspoon, scoop out small balls of filling and roll in the palm of your hands until smooth and even. Repeat until all of the filling has been used up.

Roll balls in the hazelnuts to coat them well. Store truffles in an airtight container in the fridge for up to 5 days. Bring to room temperature before serving.

12 oz (375 g) semi-sweet or bittersweet chocolate, chopped

4 large egg yolks

¼ cup plus 2 Tbsp (90 mL) butter, at room temperature

2 Tbsp (30 mL) dark rum

½ tsp (2 mL) instant coffee powder or granules

1 cup (250 mL) toasted hazelnuts, finely chopped

Makes 3 dozen.

Per truffle: 101 cals, 7.4 g fat, 3.2 g sat. fat, 48 mg cholesterol, 21 mg sodium, 6.9 g carbs, 1.6 g protein

Maple Walnut Fudge

This old-fashioned fudge is rich, creamy, and Canadian!

½ cup plus 2 Tbsp (155 mL)
canned regular evaporated milk

2 cups (500 mL) firmly packed light brown sugar

¾ cup (185 mL) unsalted butter, cut into pieces

¼ tsp (1 mL) salt

½ tsp (2 mL) vanilla

½ tsp (2 mL) Mapeleine or maple extract

1¾ cups (185 mL) icing sugar

½ cup (125 mL) toasted walnuts, chopped

Makes 64 pieces.

Per piece: 69 cals, 3 g fat, 1.5 g sat. fat, 7 mg cholesterol,
28 g sodium, 10.4 g carbs, 0.3 g protein

Bring the milk, brown sugar, butter, and salt to a boil in a 3-quart (3 L) heavy saucepan on medium heat, stirring until the sugar dissolves. Reduce heat to low and simmer, stirring frequently, until thickened to "soft ball" stage, about 30 minutes. (Test the mixture by dropping a small amount into a cup of ice water; it should form a soft, textured ball.)

Transfer to a heatproof bowl; beat in the vanilla and Mapeleine with an electric mixer on medium speed. Add the icing sugar a little at a time, beating until the fudge is thick and smooth, about 5 minutes. Add the toasted walnuts and stir to combine.

Spread evenly into an ungreased, medium, square baking pan. Chill, uncovered, until firm enough to cut, about 30 minutes. Cut into 1-inch (2.5 cm) squares with a sharp knife.

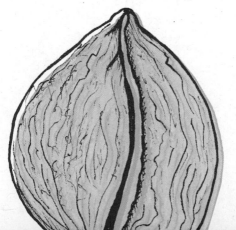

Homemade Peanut Butter Cups

No one will believe that you actually made these treats yourself so don't tell them how easy they are to prepare.

Filling

In a medium bowl, whisk the sour cream with the icing sugar until smooth. Add the cream and vanilla; mix well. Stir in the peanut butter. Cover and chill for at least 2 hours (or prepare the filling the day before). Place the chocolate cups on a baking sheet (one with sides so they don't slide off) and fill each one with 1 teaspoon (5 mL) filling.

Topping

Melt ½ cup (125 mL) chocolate dipping wafers in a bowl in the microwave on medium-low heat. Start by heating them for 2 minutes and stir. Heat for 1 minute more and stir again. Continue stirring to finish the melting. If unmelted wafers remain, heat for 30 to 60 seconds more.

Spread 1 teaspoon (5 mL) chocolate overtop of the peanut butter filling to seal it. It may take slightly more than 1 teaspoon (5 mL) for some of them. Melt more chocolate as needed. Level the tops with a knife or spatula so they look clean. Chill them to set the chocolate, about 30 minutes. Keep in an airtight container for up to 3 days in the fridge, or up to 3 months in the freezer.

Filling

¼ cup (60 mL) sour cream

⅓ cup (80 mL) icing sugar

2 Tbsp (30 mL) whipping cream

¼ tsp (1 mL) vanilla

¾ cup (185 mL) smooth peanut butter

3 3.7-oz (106 g) packages Botticelli mini Belgian chocolate cups (18 per box)

Topping

8 oz (250 g) dark chocolate dipping wafers

Makes 4 dozen.

Per confection: 91 cals, 5.4 g fat, 2.5 g sat. fat, 2 mg cholesterol, 3 mg sodium, 8.8 g carbs, 1.7 g protein

Nut Pairing Guide

Every nut has a specific taste and texture, as well as distinct characteristics. Certain foods and beverages combine particularly well with specific nuts. This guide will help you choose complementary savoury and sweet things to serve with your favourite nuts.

Almonds: *mild flavour, firm texture, strong crunch when toasted*
Savoury: mild cheeses, including cream cheeses; green vegetables; green salads with fruit; chicken; shrimp; white fish, such as sole, halibut, and cod; curries, chickpeas
Sweet: berries; tree fruit; chocolate; flaky pastries; honey; cream; mascarpone cheese; vanilla; cinnamon; nutmeg; brandy and cognac; raisins and currants; coconut; maple
Beverages: coffee; black tea; crisp white wine, such as Sauvignon Blanc; brandy and cognac; sherry

Brazil Nuts: *mild flavour, meaty, soft crunch when toasted*
Savoury: mushrooms; onions; barley; rosemary; chèvre cheese; multi-grain breads;
Sweet: caramel and toffee flavours; milk and dark chocolate; dates; coconut
Beverages: coffee; buttery white wines, such as Chardonnay; light red wines; cream ales

Cashews: *mellow flavour, soft texture, buttery, medium crunch when toasted*
Savoury: sweet and sour Asian sauces; soy sauce; sesame seeds; ginger; garlic; black pepper; chili peppers; citrus; avocado; green leafy vegetables; cucumber; snow peas; chicken; cream sauces; curries; Boursin, Havarti, Camembert, and Cambozola cheeses; French bread
Sweet: caramel; chocolate; custards; vanilla; cinnamon; coconut; lemon and lime; cream; cream cheese
Beverages: coffee; fruity white wines, such as Riesling or Gewürztraminer; pale ales

Chestnuts: *nutty smell and flavour when toasted, soft texture, smooth when puréed*
Savoury: bacon; mushrooms; onions; poultry; root vegetables; squash; smoked meats; dark rye, whole or multi-grain breads; Brie and Provolone cheeses
Sweet: dark chocolate; cream, custards, dark rum, brandy, cream cheese
Beverages: coffee; Pinot Noir, Merlot, and Beaujolais wines; Scotch ales; ciders

Hazelnuts: *robust flavour, hard crunch and nutty aroma when toasted, earthy*
Savoury: green vegetables; mustard; Emmenthal, Gruyère, Fontina, and Manchego cheeses; red meats; game; organ meats; whole-grain and dark rye breads; lentils and barley
Sweet: dark chocolate; cinnamon; orange; vanilla; cream; cream cheese; dark rum flavour; figs; dates; tree fruit; cherries; cranberries
Beverages: coffee; Cabernet Sauvignon, Shiraz, and Malbec wines; ales or bock beers; dessert wines

Macadamia Nuts: *mild taste, rich buttery texture, soft crunch when toasted*
Savoury: white fish; prawns; crab and lobster; chicken; pork; butter sauces
Sweet: tropical fruit; honey; caramel; all chocolate; coconut; cream; cream cheese; dark rum; brandy
Beverages: coffee; creamy cocktails, such as Golden Cadillac, China White and White Russian; cream liqueurs; Riesling and Gewürztraminer white wines

Peanuts: *robust taste and aroma, buttery texture, hard crunch when toasted*

Savoury: ginger; garlic; soy sauce; lime; chili peppers; lemon grass; curries; chicken; shrimp; pork; white fish; rice and rice noodles; green vegetables

Sweet: milk or dark chocolate; caramel; fudge; cream; cream cheese; oatmeal; honey

Beverages: cola soft drinks; root beer; pale ales and lagers; regular and chocolate milk; banana smoothies

Pecans: *soft meaty chew, light crunch with nutty aroma and flavour when toasted*

Savoury: sweet potatoes; corn; mushrooms; mild to sharp cheddar, Asiago, and Gruyère cheeses; white or brown breads; green salads; mild and hot chili peppers; red meats; pork; salad greens

Sweet: caramel; chocolate, honey; citrus, especially oranges; tree fruit; vanilla; dates; cinnamon; oats; raisins; coconut; cream; maple

Beverages: coffee; black tea; ales; Chardonnay, Merlot, and Pinot Noir wines; red sangria; bourbon and dark rum

Pine Nuts: *mild flavour, soft texture with a buttery finish when toasted*

Savoury: spicy dishes; chili peppers; salsa; avocado; spinach; Asian greens; tomatoes; peppers; corn; eggplant; savoury pastries; cream sauces; chicken; fish and seafood

Sweet: flaky pastries; cinnamon; vanilla; custard

Beverages: buttery Chardonnays and light red wines; sherries; light beers and cream ales

Pistachios: *soft meaty chew, medium crunch with nutty aroma and taste when toasted*

Savoury: avocado; tomatoes; spicy salsas; sweet and sour sauce; cream sauces; red meats; white fish, such as cod, snapper, and mahi mahi; mustard; havarti, Monterey Jack, and Farmer's cheeses; white French, Italian, and sourdough breads

Sweet: citrus; tropical fruits; coconut; dark chocolate; custard; cream; cream cheese

Beverages: Sauvignon Blanc and Pinot Gris wines; light beers; white sangria; lemonade; lime margaritas

Walnuts: *soft chew, slightly bitter when raw but delicate, buttery crunch when toasted*

Savoury: Pecorino, chèvre, Gorgonzola, and Cambozola cheeses; mushrooms; bacon; ham; red meats; roasted red peppers; onions; leeks; shallots

Sweet: figs; dates; honey; flaky pastries; cream; crème fraîche

Beverages: Zinfandel, Shiraz, and Cabernet Sauvignon wines; Port; dark and stout beers

Toasting and Storing Nuts

Toasting Nuts

Purpose: increases the flavour for a richer taste and crisps the texture.

Oven Method

Preheat your oven to 350°F (180°C).

Spread out the nuts, in a single layer, on a baking sheet with sides. Bake for 5 to 8 minutes, stirring at least once halfway through the cooking. Roast the nuts until golden, not dark brown, because they can taste burnt when dark. Cool on a rack at room temperature; they will crisp up as they cool.

Skillet Method

Preheat a skillet on medium heat for 2 to 3 minutes.

Add the nuts and toast them for 2 to 4 minutes, stirring almost continuously for even browning. Remove from heat and move nuts to a cool surface to crisp up.

Storing Nuts

Nuts stored in their shells have a natural protective exterior and will keep longer than shelled ones. Similarly, nuts with skins will last longer than blanched nuts.

Raw nuts go rancid easily therefore wrap them well and store in the freezer for up to 2 years or refrigerate them for up to 9 months. Toasted nuts will last for 10 to 14 days in a sealed plastic bag or a covered container.

Candied nuts will stay crisp, even in a humid climate, for up to 5 to 7 days in a covered tin. Line the tin with foil or wax paper first. Do not refrigerate. Other covered containers or bags are acceptable for storing candied nuts for up to 2 days. In humid climates, nuts or candied nuts kept in an open bowl will soften in less then 24 hours. In a dry climate, nuts or candied nuts will stay crisp for at least twice as long. Candied nuts can also be frozen; to re-crisp them, bake for 1 to 2 minutes on an oiled (or parchment-lined) baking sheet in a preheated 400°F (200°C) oven.

Nut Oils and Butters

Nut oils should be refrigerated after opening to prolong their shelf life; otherwise, they will go rancid in 9 to 12 months.

Natural nut butters have oil on top that helps prevent the air from reaching the butter. Make sure to push any butter in the jar below the oil level to seal and refrigerate for up to 1 year. You will have to bring the nut butter to room temperature to use or it will be too stiff to stir.

Blanching Nuts

Blanching removes the outer skin from the nut so it has a smooth surface and even colour.

To blanch 2 cups (500 mL) of nuts, bring a medium saucepan half-filled with water to a full boil. Add the nuts and cook for 1 minute to loosen the skins. (You can also accomplish this by pouring boiling water over nuts in a heat-proof bowl and letting them sit for 5 minutes.)

Drain the nuts and place them on a tea towel or on paper towels and cover with the same. Gently rub your hands back and forth on top of the towels to rub off the skins. Separate the skins from the nuts and discard the skins.

Almonds are available already blanched in most stores. Occasionally, you can find blanched hazelnuts in stores.

Substituting Nuts in Recipes

In general, my recipes are based on the specific flavours of ingredients, however, there are many recipes in *Go Nuts* where you can successfully substitute one kind of nut for another. The flavour may vary somewhat but the recipe will likely turn out just fine and you may prefer it made with your favourite instead. My substitutions are based on picking similar textures, crunch (hardness or softness), and flavour.

Here are some substitutions that should produce similar results in recipes, and which can be used interchangeably:

peanuts / cashews; peanut butter / cashew butter

almonds / hazelnuts; almond butter / hazelnut butter

pecans / walnuts

chestnuts are quite unique but you can use walnuts for the closest in flavor and texture

pistachios: use pecans for a similar nut flavour or pumpkin seeds for a similar texture

pine nuts: use sunflower seeds or pumpkin seeds for similar texture

Brazil nuts / Macadamia nuts for a similar nut texture and a buttery flavour

Brazil nuts: use unsweetened coconut if a meaty texture is required

Ingredient Reference List and Recommended Brands

Almond milk: Available in 4-cup (1 L) cartons. I prefer Almond Breeze by Blue Diamond. Use the unsweetened or "natural" flavour in *Go Nuts* recipes for the best results. You will find it in the canned milk section of supermarkets.

Artichoke hearts: Canned Tosca or Unico brand are fine. "No name" brands often include tough leaves that you have to discard so there's more waste.

Balsamic vinegar: The aged ones are the most expensive but taste the best. Pick one from a reputable company. Bargain brands can taste watery.

Basmati rice: Use white long-grain Indian Basmati rice and wash it 3 times or until the water runs clear.

Brown sugar: Generally use dark brown, such as Best Brown, and not demerara.

Butter: Generally use unsalted, especially for desserts. If you substitute salted, you may want to cut back on any salt in the recipe.

Chestnuts: Ready-to-use peeled, whole, cooked chestnuts are available in a 100 g package from Dan-D-Pak, a 439 g can from Clément Faugier, or a 720 g jar from Italissima. A 100 g package yields about ½ cup (125 mL) of packed, chopped chestnuts.

Chestnut purée: Available in unsweetened (479 g can) or sweetened versions (78 g tube) from Clément Faugier.

Chili–garlic sauce: Use Chinese chili–garlic sauce or substitute sambal oelek and minced garlic.

Chocolate: Specified by sweetness, i.e., Baker's semi-sweet. Other good brands are Lindt and Ghirardelli.

Cocoa: Unsweetened dark Dutch cocoa powder, available in the bulk section or the baking aisle of most grocery stores. Many brands are not dark and produce products that are lighter in colour and taste.

Dijon mustard: Use Maille or another French brand for the best flavour.

Dried pasta: Use Italian ones made with semolina, such as la Molisana, Riscossa, and Delverde.

Eggs: Large size, preferably free-range ones, especially for omelettes and egg entrées.

Extracts: Flavourings, such as vanilla, almond, or orange, should be pure extracts for the best flavour.

Flour: All-purpose white (regular or unbleached) unless otherwise specified.

Honey: Liquid honey, not solid, creamed, or crystallized honey.

Icing sugar: Also known as confectioner's sugar or powdered sugar.

Instant Asian noodles: Use 400 g packages of Rooster or Diamond brand, available in the Asian section of most grocery stores. Each package will have 7 portions of compressed noodles.

Jasmine rice: Use white long-grain Thai Jasmine rice and wash it 3 times or until the water runs clear.

Ketchup: Also known as catsup; Heinz brand suggested for recipe flavour consistency.

Light cream or cereal cream: 15% to 18% milk fat cream.

Long grain rice: Regular white converted rice but not instant.

Margarine: Block margarine may be substitued for butter if you have an allergy or dairy restriction. The recipe may taste slightly different with the margarine. Use canola- or corn-based products for the best flavour; not soybean. Be aware that hydrogenated margarines do contain trans fats.

Mayonnaise: Use Kraft Real Mayonnaise or Hellmann's mayonnaise for the best flavour.

Milk: Whole or homogenized milk (5% milk fat); otherwise specified as canned, evaporated, etc.

Nut butters: Organic peanut, almond, cashew, macadamia nut, and hazelnut butters are available in 250 mL jars from Nuts to You Nut Butter. They are located in the jam/peanut butter aisle of grocery stores. Dan-D-Pak has a similar variety of nut butters in stores and is also a Canadian company. Peanut butter used in *Go Nuts* recipes is the smooth, hydrogenated kind (i.e., Skippy) not the "natural" or "old-fashioned" kind with the oil on top.

Nut oils: Almond, peanut, and walnut oils are available from Spectrum Naturals in 375 mL bottles in the oil section of grocery stores or at organic/health food stores. There are also several California nut oil companies whose products are available in kitchen shops and delis but they are priced higher.

Olive oil: Pomace olive oil is okay for frying but use extra is virgin olive oil for dressings and drizzling.

Prawns: 16/20 or 21/30 count per pound frozen raw prawns, tail on or easy peel are preferred.

Rice vinegar: Available in the Asian section of grocery stores or substitute white vinegar.

Whole roasted red peppers: I recommend Tosca or Italissima brand. Sometimes they also stock julienned ones. Available in jars in the condiment section of grocery stores.

Sherry vinegar: Available at Italian and Spanish delis. Like fine cognac or wine, the price is determined by the number of years it has been aged; 30- to 50-year-old vinegar is far more expensive.

Stocks: Regular fat-free chicken or beef as listed, unless specified as low-sodium, especially for recipes where the product will be boiled to reduce the volume. I use regular Pacific stock or Knorr brand. If I purchase any other brands, I buy low-sodium types because they generally do not contain MSG.

Sugar: Granulated white from sugar beets or sugar cane unless another kind is specified.

Spices: Considered ground, unless otherwise specified as whole, etc.

Tomatoes: For canned ones, use crushed, diced, or whole; "no name" brands are acceptable.

Yellow sugar: Use golden sugar or light brown sugar.

Whipping cream: 32% to 35% milk fat cream.

Worcestershire sauce: Use a reputable brand, such as Heinz or HP; not a "no name" one. If you need a pure vegetarian product, without anchovy, then substitute vegetarian "Worcestershire-style" sauce, which is available in health food stores.

Metric Conversion Chart

These measurements have been rounded off and are therefore not exact. Use only as a guideline for easy calculations.

Volume Equivalents
1 tablespoon (Tbsp) = 3 teaspoons (tsp) = ½ fluid ounce (oz) =
    15 millilitres (mL)
2 Tbsp = 6 tsp = 1 oz = 30 mL
¼ cup = 4 Tbsp = 2 oz = 60 mL

⅓ cup = 5 Tbsp plus 1 tsp = 2⅔ oz = 80 mL
½ cup = 8 Tbsp = 4 oz = 125 mL
⅔ cup = 10 Tbsp plus 2 tsp = 5⅓ oz = 160 mL
¾ cup = 12 Tbsp = 6 oz = 185 mL
1 cup = 16 Tbsp = 8 oz = 250 mL
1 pint = 2 cups = 16 oz = 500 mL
1 quart = 2 pints = 4 cups = 32 oz = 1000 mL or 1L
1 gallon = 4 quarts = 8 pints = 16 cups = 128 oz = 4000 mL or 4 L

Weight Equivalents
½ pound (lb) = 8 oz = 250 grams (g)
1lb = 16 oz = 500 g
1 kilogram (kg) = 1000 g = 2 lb

Standard Baking Pan Sizes and Capacity

medium loaf pan: 8½" × 4½" × 2½"; 6 cups
large loaf pan: 9" × 5" × 3"; 8 cups
medium rectangular pan: 11" × 7" × 2"; 8 cups
large rectangular pan: 13" × 9" × 2"; 12 cups
medium square pan: 8" × 8" × 2"; 8 cups
large square pan: 9" × 9" × 2"; 10 cups
small round pan: 8" × 2"; 7 cups
medium round pan: 9" × 2"; 8 cups
deep medium pan: 9" × 3"; 12 cups

large round pan: 10" × 2"; 10 cups
medium springform pan: 9" × 2½"; 10 cups
large springform pan: 10" × 2¾"; 15 cups
medium baking sheet: 10¼" × 15¼"
large baking sheet: 11" × 17"
medium baking pan: 14½" × 10½" × 2"; 10 cups
large baking pan: 16¼" × 11¼" × 2"; 12 cups

Index

Acknowledgements

Thank you to the following people who helped make this book happen:

Ruth Linka for reading my initial proposal and being as excited about this book as I am. Her faith in this project started me down a path that I have wanted to take for many years. Her ongoing encouragement, knowledge, and patience have helped me through this new challenge.

Holland Gidney for her guidance through the editing process and teaching me better ways to express my thoughts and ideas on paper.

Pete Kohut, designer, for helping my illustrations come to life.

Everyone at TouchWood who helped to make my first book-writing experience positive, rewarding, and relatively painless.

Juanita Stein, Allan Mandell, and Rene Pelequin for being both friends and advisers to me. I treasure your professional advice and endless encouragement along the way.

Dad and Irene for always having faith in me, my projects, and my dreams.

Special thanks to Scott, Dale, Brenda, Wayne, Laura, Joel, Logan, Ashley, and Jon for being my test kitchen audience and official tasters.

And to all my friends and relatives who have donated various food products to "the cause." I have received freshly harvested fruits and vegetables from many of you as well as gourmet gifts from afar. I also appreciate your culinary inquiries that keep me on my toes.

Fish On: Seafood Dishes that Make a Splash
Ingrid Baier

978-1-926741-12-3 • $19.95

Tequila Lime Grilled Halibut
Tandoori Salmon with Mango Chutney
Crab Bisque

Just a few of the mouth-watering recipes from *Fish On*,
a seafood lover's guide to the true tastes of the Pacific.